# The Believer's Brain

About 90 percent of people have faith in a supreme being, but our yearning for the divine, and whatever it promises, involves a large divergence in mental states and behaviors. Some people adhere to doctrine, supplication, and fastidious religious practices; others have a strong sense that they are part of something greater and more universal. However, all religious and spiritual paths are mediated by complex brain networks.

When different areas of the brain are stimulated, a person can have a variety of experiences, but no specific "God spot" exists where stimulation enhances religiosity or spirituality. Functional brain imaging shows that specific areas of the brain "light up" when subjects perform certain religious activities, but imaging provides only anatomic correlations, not functional explanations.

*The Believer's Brain* takes a step beyond these singular methodologies, providing converging evidence from a variety of study methods of how humans' brain networks mediate different aspects of religious and spiritual beliefs, feelings, actions, and experiences.

Although this book reveals how our brain is the home of the religious and spiritual mind, understanding this gift will not diminish our spirituality or our love for or belief in a supreme being, but will increase appreciation of the apparatus that mediates these mental states.

**Kenneth M. Heilman**, MD, the James E. Rooks Jr. Distinguished Professor of Neurology and Health Psychology at the University of Florida, has described several new diseases and is the author or editor of 14 books, 100 textbook chapters, and 500 research journal publications about brain–behavior relations. He is listed in Best Doctors in America, America's Top Doctors, and *Who's Who*. He has trained approximately 70 postdoctoral fellows, many of whom are now leaders in neurology and neuropsychology.

**Russell S. Donda** has devoted nearly two decades to expanding and translating science into clearly understood and useful ideas. He has launched several companies and spearheaded the development of multiple novel technologies. His efforts have spawned a number of innovations, and he is an inventor on 15 patents and applications.

# The Believer's Brain

Home of the Religious
and Spiritual Mind

**Kenneth M. Heilman
and Russell S. Donda**

**Psychology Press**
Taylor & Francis Group

NEW YORK AND LONDON

First published 2014
by Psychology Press
711 Third Avenue, New York, NY 10017

and by Psychology Press
27 Church Road, Hove, East Sussex BN3 2FA

*Psychology Press is an imprint of the Taylor & Francis Group, an informa business*

*Library of Congress Cataloging-in-Publication Data*

The Believer's Brain: Home of the Religious and Spiritual Mind /
Kenneth M. Heilman and Russell S. Donda.
    pages cm
    BJ1533.R42H825    2013
    179—dc23        2013016485

ISBN: 978-1-84872-500-3 (hbk)
ISBN: 978-1-84872-501-0 (pbk)
ISBN: 978-1-315-81719-4 (ebk)

Typeset in Times
by Apex CoVantage, LLC

MIX
Paper from
responsible sources
FSC
www.fsc.org    FSC® C014174

Printed and bound in the United States of America by Sheridan Books, Inc. (a Sheridan Group Company).

# Contents

# Figures

# Preface

When we pray fervently, beseech God, sing in our place of worship, become enraptured in a biblical story, defend our religious beliefs, or do other things related to our religion, what neural networks in the brain are most active? Which are not? What is our brain doing when, rather than performing some religious activity, we are having a mystical or transcendent experience? Are different parts of the brain engaged then? This book is about how those things happen—how the brain enables humans to be religious and spiritual.

For our purposes in this book, we distinguish between "mind" and "brain." There is a long-running argument for, and against, a mind-brain dichotomy. If this book engaged in that debate, it would divert you from our main theme. So we will simply define the human brain as the organ in the skull composed of nerve cells (neurons) and glial cells, which provide those neurons with metabolic and structural support. Our brains analyze and interpret incoming sensory information from our bodies as well as the external world. The brain also stores and manipulates knowledge and allows planning and the creation of programmed actions. The mind, in contrast, consists of our memories, thoughts, ideas, and feelings. The brain, however, stores these memories and develops thoughts and feelings—even the love we feel in our hearts.

The term *religion* most often denotes a belief in one or more supernatural entities and an adherence to the teachings and laws of this entity (or entities). Often, such laws have been set down or interpreted by exemplary leaders and prophets such as Moses, Saint Paul, Muhammad, Siddhartha Gautama, and Joseph Smith. The laws also have been recorded in holy books like the Torah, the New Testament, the Quran, the Book of Mormon, and the Vedas. The actual definition of religion, however, has been debated and discussed for several thousand years. The term may come from the Latin term *relegere*, which means "to treat carefully." Alternatively, it may be derived from the word *religati*, which means "to bind." Certainly, religion does involve binding oneself to a supernatural entity or God, as well as to that God's laws. Also, sharing beliefs and following the same path can bind people together and foster a sense of community. For some people, this means associating not only with God and with people of similar faith but also with God's creation.

Although more descriptions lie in the pages ahead, we will say for now that we view religiosity as the degree of adherence to a religion; we consider "spirituality" or being "spiritual" as a state of awareness of the divine that transcends the physical world, including our corporeal bodies and its five senses.

From the beginning of recorded history to the present, much of humanity has believed in the existence of a supernatural deity or deities with supernatural powers. Diverse groups of people give the sovereign deity different names and attributes; some are anthropomorphic, others more abstract. In the mystic traditions of the world's major religions—the belief systems we would consider spiritual—a common thread weaves its way through distinct and widely separated cultures: the idea that the unknowable God is everywhere and is everything, including us.

Although we believe that some of the ideas expressed in this book are cutting-edge, this certainly is not the first book to examine the relationship between the brain and our yearning for the divine. William James (1842–1910), a Harvard Medical School graduate, is in many respects the founder of modern psychology. Many psychologists consider his book *Principles of Psychology* (Henry Holt, 1890) the "bible" of this new science. James was one of the first modern scientists to investigate religious experience as a psychological phenomenon. In *Varieties of Religious Experience,* he defined religion as "the feelings, acts and experiences of individual men . . . so far as they apprehend themselves to stand in relation to whatever they may consider divine" (2009, 31). James suggested that in order to learn about the psychology of religion, we have to study people's religious experiences. That is something on which we shed a bit of light in the pages to follow.

Psychology and psychiatry are the study of the mind, and neurology the study of the brain, in health and disease. Neuropsychology is the study of the relationship between the mind and the brain—or how the brain mediates behaviors, thoughts, emotions, and beliefs. Our goal in this book is to examine the neuropsychology of religiosity and spirituality.

In the preface to his internationally best-selling book *The God Delusion* (Bantam Books, 2006), Richard Dawkins defines a delusion as a persistent false belief held in the face of strong contradictory evidence. He then quotes Robert M. Pirsig, the author of *Zen and the Art of Motorcycle Maintenance: An Inquiry into Values* (William Morrow & Company, 1974) who wrote, "When one person suffers from a delusion, it is called insanity. When many people suffer from a delusion it is called Religion" (Dawkins, 2006, 28). Unlike Dawkins's book and others by Sam Harris and Daniel Dennett that promote atheism, as well as the multitude of books that espouse belief in a supernatural sovereign, *The Believer's Brain* strives to be theologically neutral.

We suspect that some very religious readers will interpret what we have written as promoting atheism or agnosticism. Similarly, some nonbelievers will view this book as promoting religion or spirituality. We have, though, attempted to steer our writing down the middle of the road, so that we neither support nor refute a belief in God. Equally important, we have tried to build our arguments not necessarily to terminate in answers but to prompt the reader to think and reflect on possibilities.

Perhaps some people will assert that the reason the brain can mediate faithful behavior is that God made it so. Others, basing their argument on Darwinian principles, may suggest that the reason that humanity's belief in God survives is that it increases our probability of survival. But that is difficult to accept since organized religion has been responsible for some of the most horrible events in history. Perhaps some would agree with the paleontologist and evolutionary biologist Stephan Jay Gould, who called religion a spandrel: an evolutionary trait that, on its own, has no adaptive value.

In their book *The Spiritual Brain* (HarperCollins, 2007), Mario Beauregard and Denyse O'Leary discuss an important philosophical question: did God create the brain, or does the brain create God? They do not provide any evidence to resolve this question, and neither do we. Nor are we sure that it can ever be resolved. In the end, irrespective of how any of us might answer this question, it is the brain that permits us to be religious or spiritual.

In the article "Darwin's God" in the *New York Times Magazine* (March 4, 2007), Robin Marantz Henig writes, "In the world of evolutionary biology, the question is not whether God exists, but why we believe in him." Although Henig says that scholars agree that religious belief is an outgrowth of brain architecture, this article does not discuss the brain architecture that might mediate such belief. The opposite is true of this book; we discuss, in fair detail, some of the brain systems that might mediate certain elements of our religiosity and spirituality.

The brain is the most complex organ of our body, and despite many years of research, much is still poorly understood. Accordingly, we can offer little insight on many aspects of religiosity and spirituality. In the evolution of science, numerous theories have eventually been proven to be incorrect; similarly, we know that many of the explanations in the pages to follow will be faulted. However, the development of a knowledge system is evolutionary. As in biological evolution, each step in the acquisition of knowledge is not perfect but each draws us ever closer to a fuller understanding.

This book has two authors. Ken Heilman is an academic physician and neuroscientist. Russ Donda is a translationalist, a person who finds the value in and seeks to commercialize science. Not only have we been educated differently, we also have divergent religious and cultural backgrounds. When writing this book, we sometimes disagreed about what to include or withhold. Fortunately, we do agree on most of what ultimately has been included; however, some sections in Chapter 7, especially "The Wolves Are Outside" are exceptions. Russ wished them to be excluded; however, Ken insisted on inclusion.

Nevertheless, we endeavored to write this book so that those of us who are not physicians or neuroscientists will understand it. But when describing the brain's architecture and functions, we have used many technical terms to denote and describe those structures and their functions. We have tried to use these terms in a way that is not too tedious; the figures should also help.

Throughout this book we use the terms *we*, *us*, and *our* to refer to humanity collectively, but, because we are the coauthors, we also use them for our singular author's voice. We think it usually will be clear when *we* mean the author's voice and when it does not; if it is not clear, it probably does not need to be. When talking about one of us in particular, we use our first names, Ken or Russ. Regarding the use of *he* or *she* in the pages to follow, gender does not really matter, and we do our best to alternate between pronouns. However, sometimes we have felt it necessary to stress that *he* and *she* should be viewed equivalently in the context of this book, and both are then used.

Ultimately, we hope that after reading this book, you will have a better understanding of the brain mechanisms that might account for our religiosity and spirituality. Although much will remain unexplained, if we have provided you with some new understandings and prompted you to think, to question, and to be even more curious, we have done our job.

# 1 Introduction

## A World of Believers

*The belief in God has often been advanced as not only the greatest, but the most complete of all the distinctions between man and the lower animals. It is however impossible, as we have seen, to maintain that this belief is innate or instinctive in man. On the other hand a belief in all-pervading spiritual agencies seems to be universal; and apparently follows from a considerable advance in man's reason, and from a still greater advance in his faculties of imagination, curiosity and wonder.*

—Charles Darwin, *The Descent of Man*

### Everywhere, Naturally?

We yearn for the divine. On a planet of 6.9 billion people, a full 6 billion of us practice some form of religion. Christians, Muslims, and Hindus make up two-thirds of the total; the remaining 1.4 billion practice Buddhism, Shinto, Sikhism, Judaism, the Bahá'í Faith, and various folk religions. In all, 87 percent of humans profess a belief in some supernatural deity. This is a compelling number.

Is this ocean of faith in something invisible and intangible a throwback to some more primal longing? No, not if a relatively upscale lifestyle is any gauge. Consider this: In the United States, a country that ranks among the highest in the world with regard to technological advancement, a nation with a standard of living envied by much (if not all) of the world, nearly its entire population—9 out 10 people—believes in God; 84 percent say that they engage in "conversational prayer" in which they talk with God in their own words.[1] In a Gallup poll, 59 percent state that religion plays an "important role" in their life.[2]

Primal or not, believing in some supernatural deity apparently is at least a very old practice. In *The World's Religions*, Houston Smith says that for the bulk of human history, religions were present, but oriented around the tribe. When we look at cave art, carvings, and the remains of prehistoric humans accompanied by various burial objects, it is easy to see that our early ancestors might have believed in some kind of deity and afterlife.

But artifacts, symbols, and iconography are really all that we have; we do not know what our ancient ancestors thought about religion. In today's world, direct sensory experiences with God or the divine are not widely published; those who claim literal encounters often show other signs of mental illness. And although the Bible and other holy books tell stories of individuals, such as Moses, who are said to have directly communicated with God, such accounts yield a range of metaphorical and literal interpretations. It is probably safe to say that the vast majority of people who believe in God do not have Moses-like experiences. Yet we remain faithful.

It might sound like a far-fetched comparison, but think about this: most of us have never had a firsthand experience of Antarctica, yet we completely trust that it is there because we have hard evidence of its existence. In a world driven by the realities of what we can confirm with our five senses, why we continue to have faith in some unseen God is a puzzle. In *The Descent of Man*, Darwin suggests a belief in supernatural beings that have power over the cosmos is universal. In his book *Timeless Healing*, Herbert Benson of the Harvard Medical School's Mind/Body Institute says there has never been a civilization that did not believe in a God, Gods, or some supernatural force.

Perhaps these things are true. But a type of faith that defies the five senses, is universally believed, and spans cultures, geographies, and time suggests something worthy of our consideration: believing may not be entirely learned—some of it, somehow, might be hard-wired naturally into our brains.

Even if such faith were innate, the world's religions are still a diverse mix of beliefs and practices. But they also have underlying similarities, especially regarding creation and belief in a powerful, omnipresent deity. Admittedly, we often seem to focus on why a certain religious affiliation is different or not on the right path; sad to say, we even dehumanize and oppress others on the basis of their beliefs. But despite diversity, our physiology and the role the brain plays in our heavenly yearnings and convictions are all, humanly, very much the same.

Something else that we do also is humanly the same: we talk. The famous linguist Noam Chomsky says our ability to use human language is innate, and although words of similar meaning from different cultures and countries often sound different, certain fundamental principles of communication are shared by people the world over.

Several years ago, Ken received a call from a person who was writing an article for one of the Christian magazines. Apparently the caller wanted a neurologist somehow to support the notion that God made humans speak in different languages. A discussion ensued about the Tower of Babel and how, after the Great Flood, all people spoke a common language. It seems that Nimrod, Babylon's king, along with his people, decided to build a tower that was so tall it would reach into heaven. Not pleased with such arrogance, the God of the Old Testament punished humanity by confounding the common language: he made diverse groups of people use different words for the same concepts. Of course, the result was that the groups could not understand each other. But we now know that is not the end of the story—there is more to talking than just the meaning of words.

More than words, often *how* we say something most effectively conveys our intentions. Language communicates not only ideas (what we call propositional speech), but also emotions and feelings through alterations in pitch, loudness, and timing. Similarly, facial expressions can announce our sentiments. In an important study in 1969, the psychologists Paul Ekman and Wallace V. Friesen demonstrated that people isolated from other cultures could still understand apparently universal, emotional facial expressions. Expressions conveying anger, sadness, happiness, surprise, disgust, and fear without words are understood across societies. Ken told this writer that whereas humanity may have been punished for building the Tower of Babel, God did not alter this universal and fundamental means of communicating.

So if emotional expressions are transcultural, there is a high probability that they are not entirely learned, but rather, in part, are hard wired in the brain and is genetically transmitted from parent to child. We are suggesting the same for the human belief in God.

Although people all over the world use propositional speech and emotional communication, one could argue that many people do not believe in God or are agnostic; therefore, the capacity for such belief is not universal. But that is a premature conclusion. Some people decide to live their lives in silence, and many portray little emotion through their speech. This abstention from speech or near absence of emotion in speech does not mean that these capacities are not innate. We might even see strident atheists and agnostics knocking on wood or crossing their fingers.

## The God Spot: Searching for the Seat of the Soul

For the most part, the anatomy and physiology of the brain determine how it functions. And both of those are governed primarily by genetics. Because a majority of people in almost all cultures believe in a God or Gods, and have done so throughout recorded history, it seems likely that such a faith is similarly genetically determined: the sophisticated network of neural interconnections that regulate what and how we believe is, at least partially, passed from parent to child.

We do not know exactly where in the brain such a religious-belief network would be located or how it might work. It is not clear how such a "God spot" induces faith in the supernatural or motivates the religious behaviors that can accompany believing. Moreover, we do not really understand why these networks might have formed in the first place. Admittedly, there is a lot we have not yet grasped.

Hippocrates and other ancient physicians were aware that injury and disease in different parts of the brain could cause varying behavioral symptoms. So we have known for centuries that particular regions of the brain have specific functions. But the source of our belief in the supernatural has remained a mystery. In the seventeenth century, René Descartes was one of the first to look for what he considered the "seat of soul."

Definitions of the soul abound. For some religions, it embodies our spiritual nature, that part of us that continues to exist after death. Descartes believed that the soul was the container for all of the information pouring into our brains, that all thought and action arose from it. Working from a fundamental understanding of anatomy, he surmised that the soul was located at the center of the brain in a structure called the pineal (Figure 1.1). Although Descartes thought the pineal was the seat of the soul, scientists have discovered that this gland produces melatonin, important in sleeping and waking patterns.

Descartes, of course, did not have the benefit of modern imaging technologies such as computer tomography (CT) or magnetic resonance imaging (MRI). But neither did Ken when he was a medical intern at Bellevue Hospital in the early 1960s (although x-rays were being used). Descartes, then, might have appreciated a certain story from Ken's training days.

A middle-aged, comatose man had just arrived at the emergency room. The resident and Ken, the intern on call, were quite concerned that this fellow might have some kind of mass, such as a blood clot or tumor, dangerously pushing on his brain. They used an ophthalmoscope to look inside his eyes, expecting to see a bulging optic nerve as evidence of such a mass. But there was no such

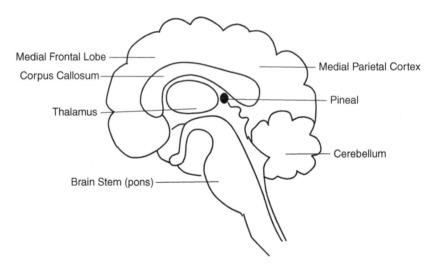

*Figure 1.1* The pineal gland. If the brain is divided into two equal halves from front to back, such that the left hemisphere is separated from the right, this would be a midsagittal section. In this section the pineal gland, in the middle of the brain, can be seen. If the pineal was calcified and an x-ray of a normal person's skull was taken, the pineal would appear here, in the middle. But if the person had a tumor or blood clot, the pineal would be pushed away from its central position.

indication with this patient; they would have to try something else. Injecting a special dye into an artery leading to the brain could facilitate observation, but that would take time—too much time. In addition, serious complications, such as stroke, can result from this procedure.

The resident asked Ken to take the patient to x-ray to shoot some cranial images. This was to see if the pineal gland had been moved out of it midline position by any impinging mass. But the resident also gave Ken some specific instructions, which Ken found interesting: "Tell the x-ray technician that if this fellow's x-rays do not show a calcified pineal, then image him again, but rotate his head during the procedure." Ken recalls that while hurriedly pushing the patient on a gurney, he asked the resident why they needed to do this. The resident explained: "If the pineal, which is in the middle of the head, is calcified, you can see it on the x-ray. However, if it is not calcified, we won't see it unless we rotate his head. In other words, everything in the x-ray will be blurred because you are moving it—except for the relatively still, center point of rotation." Pretty clever, but four hundred years ago, this would not have been news to Descartes: he, too, knew the pineal was located in the center of the head.

Recall that in addition to knowing the pineal gland's location, Descartes also believed that the soul and our thoughts, ideas, and actions emanated from this spot. But around that same period, an early pioneer in anatomical brain research, the British physician Thomas Willis (1621–1675), was thinking something else.

Willis, the founder of the British Royal Society, was one of the first people to use the term *neurology*. He was also at the forefront of exploring the functional changes associated with diseases of the brain and identified a number of the essential blood vessels. Even today, in a testament to his competence, we refer to the vasculature at the base of the brain as the Circle of Willis. In his estimation, having a clear understanding of the brain was key to penetrating the soul; studying it could "unlock the secret places of Man's Mind and [give us a] look into the living and breathing Chapel of the Deity."

Unlike Descartes, Willis thought that God had placed the soul in the corpus callosum—the central structure that joins, and enables communication between, the left and right hemispheres of the brain (see Figure 1.2). Today, we know that the corpus callosum performs a very critical function, but why Willis thought the soul was located here is a bit of a puzzle.

Long after Willis's death, studies conducted in the early twentieth century suggested that when the corpus callosum is injured, we will often see evidence of something called a hemispheric *disconnection syndrome*. In such a disconnection, each side of the brain acts independent of the other, giving rise to certain peculiar behaviors. Perhaps Willis observed something like this with one or more of his patients.

Apart from injury, the corpus callosum is sometimes intentionally severed. Some patients have severe epileptic seizures that cannot be controlled with medication. One means of stopping the spread of such attacks from one side

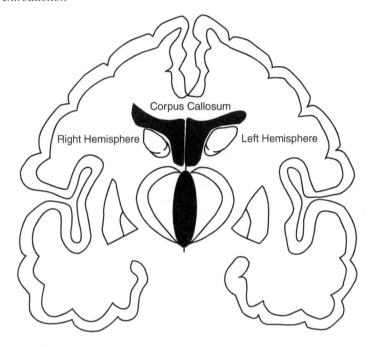

*Figure 1.2* The corpus callosum. This drawing of the brain is a coronal section. If a
         knife is used to cut the brain downward from side to side (e.g., right to left),
         the result is a coronal section. This section reveals the corpus callosum, the
         major cable connecting the right and left hemispheres.

of the brain to the other is to separate the hemispheres surgically. In this type
of surgery, the entire corpus callosum is severed. Without doubt, it is a serious procedure, and afterward the ability of one hemisphere to communicate
with the other is severely limited. Several years ago Ken had the opportunity
to examine Ellen, a woman who had undergone such a procedure for seizure
control. When he asked Ellen if she had any problems now, post-surgery, she
told him, "Sometimes my two hands get into arguments."

Ellen explained. Several days earlier, she had been wearing a red dress; when
she reached into the closet with her right hand for her matching red shoes, her
left hand suddenly pulled the shoes from her right hand, put them back on the
rack, and selected blue shoes. Because she wanted the red shoes to go with her
dress, her right hand took the blue shoes from her left—and again selected the
red shoes. But as she was picking them up her left hand slammed the closet
door on her right hand![3]

This was, of course, a puzzle to her. But Ken knew what was happening. It's
called *alien hand syndrome*. Ken explained to her how each hand is controlled
by the opposite side of the brain—the right hand by the left hemisphere and the
left hand by the right hemisphere. It seems that whereas Ellen's left hemisphere
was picking the shoes that matched her dress, her right hemisphere appears to
have preferred the color blue. Because the connection between the halves had

been severed, they could no longer communicate—and just as two countries that do not trade or communicate are more likely to go to war than those with well-established ties, Ellen's two hemispheres engaged in a battle.

But was Ellen's experience a result of epilepsy or of the severing of her corpus callosum?

A callosal disconnection can also occur with strokes, and in 1983, Bob Watson and Ken reported that alien hand syndrome can result from strokes in the absence of epilepsy. If Thomas Willis observed this type of alien hand behavior along with corpus callosum injury, he might have thought it a confirmation of a fractured soul. Indeed, and perhaps not surprisingly, the corpus callosum is located in the midsagittal plane, the line dividing the head and brain into equal-sized right and left halves—not far from Descartes's "soul" in the pineal gland.

## A New Lens on the God Spot: Functional Imaging

Research into the God spot still is happening today. In a sense, this continuing quest is a part of our yearning for the divine. But now there is good news. The search methods have vastly improved as a result of a sophisticated exploratory tool: functional imaging.

Not all the areas of the brain are active at the same time. When a part of the brain is active, nerve cells—*neurons*—work by "firing." At rest, a nerve cell, like a battery, maintains an electrical potential, but when it becomes active, or fires, an electrical impulse is created and travels to other cells. In some circumstances, the firing rate of neurons might be as rapid as 100 times per second. After a neuron fires, it has to reestablish or rebuild its charge so it can repeat the process. The neuron does this by actively pumping some charged sodium ions from inside to outside the cell, and conversely letting charged potassium ions into the cell. The neuron requires fuel in order to do this; in humans, that energizing fuel is the sugar (glucose) and oxygen carried in the blood. It is clear that when a part of the brain is active, it receives more blood and uses more glucose. By imaging and measuring the change in blood flow or the uptake of glucose in different parts of the brain, neuroscientists are learning what areas of the brain have increased activity when we are contemplating any number of things. For example, a participant in an imaging study may be asked to think about a given topic or emotional experience.

The two most commonly used imaging technologies are positron emission tomography (PET) and functional magnetic resonance imaging (fMRI). PET involves the injection of radioisotopic markers, such as glucose, that are visual indicators of increased need for fuel. The radioisotopes tend to concentrate in the regions of greatest activity, emitting a form of radiation that PET can detect. This radiation is then used to produce a corresponding image of the brain.

fMRI works somewhat differently and does not involve injecting a radioisotope. It is based on the fact that when blood carries oxygen and glucose to active parts of the brain, the blood usually brings more fuel than can be immediately used. As a result, these active areas hold more oxygenated blood than the inactive portions. The oxygenated blood has distinct magnetic properties that the fMRI can detect and convert to images. These images provide investigators with a graphic picture of the brain's active areas.

Blood vessels are the roadways that carry fueled blood to the brain, but unlike real roads, the blood vessels can dilate to allow greater blood flow when more glucose and oxygen are needed. What's more, the brain control systems do such a superb job of road widening that often more blood is delivered than is needed. Hence, we get the increase in circulation that is visible in functional imaging.

Modern brain imaging is a phenomenal technology. A 2008 study by Beauregard and Paquette involving Carmelite nuns exemplifies how this technology can provide important information about brain function. Because the spiritual focus of the Carmelite order is contemplative prayer, the researchers must have hoped that the nuns would be good subjects for their investigation of the God spot.

While being imaged with fMRI, the nuns were asked to pray, to try and sense the presence of God. These captured images were then compared with images taken when the nuns were not praying. What the researchers found was that many areas of the brain seemed to be engaged during the prayer experience. But one place in particular—the ventromedial, or lower middle, portion of the frontal lobes (Figure 1.3)—was most active.

This finding is quite interesting, because the ventromedial region of the frontal lobes also has an association with depression. Convincing evidence for

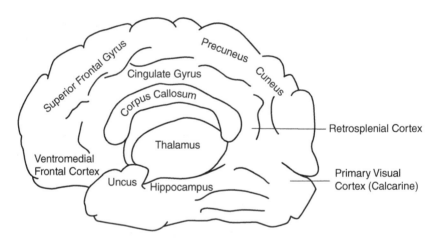

*Figure 1.3* A midsagittal section through the corpus callosum, which connects the left and right hemispheres of the brain. When the corpus callosum is divided and the hemispheres are separated, the structures on the medial surface of the brain can be seen. These structures include: the ventromedial frontal cortex, the medial portion of the superior frontal gyrus, the cingulate gyrus, the precuneus and cuneus (portions of the medial parietal lobe), the retrosplenial cortex, the primary visual (calcarine) cortex and medial parts of the temporal lobe, including the uncus and hippocampus.

this association came when Helen S. Mayberg, a Professor of Psychiatry and Behavioral Sciences and Neurology at Emory University, and her coworkers attempted to treat patients with refractory depression. This type of depression cannot be helped by psychotherapy, medications, or even electric convulsive treatment (popularly known as "electroshock therapy"). Surgically placing electrodes in the ventromedial (medial orbitofrontal) lobes and stimulating these electrodes, they discovered that many of the patients experienced reduced levels of depression.

We can guess that when the nuns were sensing the presence of God, it was a rewarding and even an euphoric experience. The finding that this same part of the brain can be stimulated to relieve depression suggests that the ventromedial portion of the frontal lobes have an important influence on mood. Unfortunately, we do not why this region controls positive and negative moods and emotions. We do know, however, that many of the medications that relieve depression increase the cellular response to a neurotransmitter called serotonin. As we mentioned, a firing neuron can influence the activity of other nearby neurons. It does so by giving off chemicals called *neurotransmitters*. Serotonin is one such neurotransmitter.

The neurons that produce serotonin happen to be in an area of the brain stem known as the raphe nuclei (see Figure 1.4). It is curious that the part of the frontal lobes that are most engaged during the nuns' prayers appears to send neural

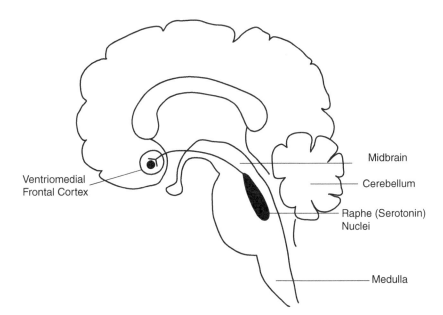

*Figure 1.4* The ventromedial frontal cortex. This midsagittal section through the corpus callosum shows the ventromedial frontal cortex, which connects with the raphe nucleus, in the brain stem. The raphe nucleus contains neurons that give off serotonin.

projections to the raphe nuclei. With activation of the frontal cortex, cells in the raphe nuclei may increase their production of serotonin (Figure 1.4). Thus, when the nuns felt the presence of God and their frontal lobes were activated, their levels of pleasure-enhancing serotonin may have increased. We know that the frontal lobes have connections to many other areas of the brain, including the nucleus accumbens—which, as we will soon see, plays an important role in our sense of reward.

So are the frontal lobes—specifically the ventromedial or orbitomedial portion—the God spot? The functional imaging studies of the praying nuns showed that many other regions of the brain were active. Does this imply that there might not be a single God spot? Might the evidence instead point to a more widely distributed network within the brain as the seat of the soul?

Certainly, we are fortunate to have functional imaging as a new kind of lens and to have learned what we did, for example, about our Carmelite nuns. But this imaging, as amazing as it sounds, is not without its drawbacks. Investigators may misinterpret the information it provides.

Consider what can happen when people are surgically treated for epilepsy by having a portion of their left brain removed. This procedure is performed if the seizures cannot be controlled adequately through medication. Epileptic seizures often start in the medial portions of the temporal lobe (including the hippocampus and amygdala) (Figure 1.5).

When these areas are surgically extracted, often seizures are dramatically reduced or even eliminated. When the section removed is the left medial temporal lobe (including the hippocampus), the patients will often display a

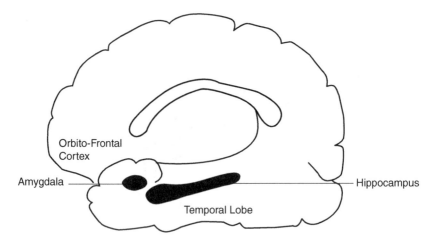

*Figure 1.5* Epileptogenic areas. These are portions of the medial temporal lobe where temporal lobe seizures often start, including the area important for memory (hippocampus), the area important in the experience of fear and anger (amygdala). In the anterior (front) portion of the temporal lobe there is another area important in smell (uncus), which can also be an area where seizures can start.

particular kind of verbal memory loss. For example, after being given several simple words to remember and then being intentionally distracted for a few minutes, the patients are unable to recall those several words. However, if the right medial temporal lobe with the hippocampus is taken out, these patients may have a spatial memory problem and be impaired when recalling faces or pictures.

With such a drastic postsurgical side effect, we might expect the left medial temporal lobe and hippocampus to be visibly active with functional imaging when a normal person is asked to recall some words. But a 1992 study by Larry Squire, a Professor of Psychiatry, Neurosciences, and Psychology at the University of California, San Diego, along with his coworkers revealed the unexpected. When healthy, normal subjects were given words to remember while being imaged, the right hippocampus appeared to be more active than the left. Was something wrong here? Squire was aware of the literature describing how removal of the left ventromedial temporal lobe and hippocampus leads to a verbal memory deficit. So without refuting this extensive literature, he and his colleagues drew an alternative explanation. They suggested that the right hippocampus became activated because, unlike the left hippocampus, it was not accustomed to performing this test of verbal memory; thus, it simply had to work harder than the left hippocampus.

In other words, Squire and his coworkers' explanation is based on the understanding that when a part of the brain is confronted with a new task, something that it is unaccustomed to performing, at first it becomes highly activated. With continued performance and increased proficiency, the level of neural activation progressively decreases.

Such observations caution us not to jump to conclusions when we observe focal activation during imaging. Seeing activity may mean that part of the brain regulates or mediates a particular function. Or it could simply indicate that the mental activity underway is not ordinarily performed by this portion of the brain and that the activated portion of the brain, unaccustomed to such a task, is working harder to perform it.

Functional imaging has other challenges. A number of interacting places in the brain perform more than a single function. When a study subject is given a particular mental task, interactions between different portions can spur observable activity that is not necessarily conclusive. We see the activity, but exactly what function is being engaged?

If you Google "functional imaging" or "fMRI" plus "cingulate gyrus," you will get several thousand hits for articles and publications. Why? Because this part of the brain (see Figure 1.3), besides its other roles, is actively employed whenever normal people perform any variety of tasks. In 1972, Ken, along with Ed Valenstein, at the University of Florida, College of Medicine, reported how the anterior portion of the cingulate gyrus plays an important role in mediating attention. For example, if the right side of this cingulate gyrus is damaged, then that person will be inattentive to stimuli coming from the left side. Thus, when a normal person in an imaging study is performing a prescribed task and we see activation of the anterior portion cingulate gyri, we do not know if the increased activity is directly relevant to the cognitive activities need for the task or if it is simply a result of the subject's paying attention to the stimuli provided with this task

We should keep in mind one additional, confounding factor. Many neurons in the brain are *inhibitory*—they stop or prevent certain processes from occurring. Conversely, other neurons are *excitatory*—they incite or sustain certain processes. If an area of the brain becomes activated during a task, we do not always know whether it is engaged in an excitatory role or an equally active inhibitory one.

The truth, though, is that, as we continue our explorations of the brain, functional imaging, despite its challenges, will allow us profound advantages over the limited resources available to Descartes and Willis. Some of those advantages will become apparent in the pages ahead.

## Notes

1. Pew Research Center, *The Global Religious Landscape: A Report on the Size and Distribution of the World's Major Religious Groups as of 2010.* December 18, 2012. http://www.pewforum.org/files/2012/12/globalReligion-full.pdf
2. Based on Gallup polls, July 29, 2003, and June 3, 2011.
3. A callosal disconnection and a resulting alien hand syndrome can occur with strokes, too, even in the absence of epilepsy like Ellen's. In the 1980s, Bob Watson and Ken showed this to be the case. Robert T. Watson and Kenneth M. Heilman, "Callosal Apraxia," *Brain* 106, pt. 2 (June 1983): 391–403.

# 2  Beliefs

## How Our Brains Get Molded and Beliefs Become Ingrained

*Train up a child the way he should go; and when he is old, he will not depart from it.*

—Proverbs 22:6

### The Impressionable, Youthful Brain

When we talk with people who are religious, and when we hear related reports and stories, it is evident that many people view their religion alone as the one, true path to the divine. Indeed, sociological studies reveal that most people do not engage in, or experience, multiple paths of belief. Children born to Christian parents, for example, are most often Christian as adults. Likewise, those born to Jewish or Muslim families tend to remain with their faiths. Yes, conversions do occur, especially in the case of love and marriage between couples of differing religions. But the imparting of particular beliefs and tenets, for the most, arises within the framework of the family.

Growing children go through an extended period when their minds are quite impressionable. During this time, exposure to family beliefs, mores, and practices can ultimately—and compellingly—influence their behavior as adults. A Christian Web site offering a Sunday school curriculum drives this point home, "You are making an eternal difference," it says, "week after week."

One of the most famous early demonstrations of just how impressionable an immature brain can be comes from Konrad Lorenz's studies of young geese. Lorenz, an Austrian zoologist and animal psychologist, noted that goslings naturally follow their mother because she is the first moving thing these little geese see.

This kind of "follow the leader" behavior likely evolved because it helped ensure the youngsters' chances for survival. After all, the mother will naturally lead them toward food and away from danger. To test this hypothesis, Lorenz conducted a now-famous study. He carefully placed goose eggs in an incubator so that within hours of hatching, the babies were exposed not to their mother, but to Lorenz. Subsequently, when the youngsters saw Lorenz walking away, they followed him as if he were their mother. Their brains, young and impressionable, were imprinted with Lorenz as their parent figure (Figure 2.1).

This may lead us to ask, if a form of this imprinting also happens in human children? Some psychologists suggest that it does not. But there is growing evidence to the contrary, and even some of our simplest activities seem to confirm that imprinting occurs. How many of us learned as children to brush our teeth before bed each night and, as adults, are pretty uncomfortable when, while traveling, we get to the hotel and discover we forgot to pack a toothbrush? Chances are, we will figure out how to get a toothbrush pretty quickly.

A lot of people call such behaviors habits; however, the term *habit* simply describes a frequently repeated behavior. It does not explain fully why a person

*Figure 2.1* Konrad Lorenz being followed by baby geese. Immediately after hatching, these goslings saw Lorenz, rather than their mother, walk away from them and followed him around as if he were their mother.

continually performs the same activity. In Lorenz's view, behaviors that become imprinted are learned under a unique set of circumstances—unlike learning by exposure to events or objects that elicit or prompt a particular behavior. This latter phenomenon, commonly referred to as associative learning, is similar to imprinting, but imprinting requires a unique condition: Lorenz (1970 and 1971) said that age is key—imprinting must take place during a critical period in the growth and maturation of the brain. Otherwise, it will not occur. In contrast, associative learning can take place at any time in life. Indeed, if a certain behavioral or learning pattern is not imprinted by a certain age, it may never be fully learned. Additionally, unlike associative learning, imprinting seems to be difficult to abate and is not easily reversed—if at all.

In studying zebra finches, Fernando Nottebaum, of the Rockefeller University Field Research Center, along with his coworkers, observed how younger birds learned to sing by imitating mature finches. The researchers wondered what might happen if there was a delay in the youngsters' exposure to the elders' songs. So they kept two generations apart until the youngsters were 65 days old. Of course, because of this separation, they were not exposed to the older finches' songs.

What the researchers discovered is quite interesting. First of all, coming out of the forced separation, the younger generation was unable to sing like normal zebra finches. Even after hearing the older birds sing, they still could not develop their natural vocal abilities. They had lost the ability to be imprinted.

Why did the young birds have this learning deficit? There is evidence that the hormone testosterone alters the neural networks responsible for learning such songs; after the testosterone level increases in a maturing finch's brain, the bird loses the ability to learn what would appear to be innate. We suspect that the neural networks storing this information lose their plasticity—their capacity to change. The networks become fixed and nearly incapable of change, even after exposure to new stimuli, such as, in this case, the zebra finch's natural song.

One example of evidence of age-related imprinting in humans is our ability to learn a new language. Prepubescent children who immigrate to a country where a different language is spoken can often learn to speak this new language without any accent. However, those who emigrate after puberty, and then learn the language, typically will talk with an accent. Henry Kissinger is an excellent example of this phenomenon. Born in Germany in 1923, he came to the United States in 1938, when he was about 15 years old. Kissinger was 50 years old when he became secretary of state in 1973. Although he had lived in America for 35 years, as many of us know he still had a thick, northern Bavarian accent.

## Making Memories

We do not know exactly how early-age imprinting takes place. What we have discovered, however, is that learning and forming memories does not simultaneously involve the entire brain. There are several different forms of memory, and each is processed in different parts of the brain. Consider the famous and interesting case of Henry Gustav Molaison (1926–2008), better known as "H.M." He suffered from medically intractable epilepsy and, later, a profound episodic memory disorder.

When neurons are active—that is, firing—the brain emits small electrical currents. Neurologists use electroencephalography, EEG for short, to amplify these currents emanating from the brain and using this apparatus, they can locate the seizure focus, the area of the brain that is source of the problem. Normally, the electrical recordings from the brain (EEG) are reminiscent of gentle ocean waves on a calm day. However, during a seizure, on the EEG the brain waves become agitated, not unlike that same ocean during a storm. Epilepsy commonly is caused by an abnormality in the cerebral cortex, particularly in the medial portion of the temporal lobes (Figure 1.5). With this kind of temporal lobe epilepsy, the neurons in the anterior portion of medial temporal lobe will periodically discharge in an irregular fashion. This unusual, frenetic activity can spread to other areas in the brain; when this happens, a seizure occurs. Unfortunately, these dangerous and debilitating attacks are often impossible to control fully with antiepileptic medications. When that is the case, surgery is often recommended. This surgery, which removes the part of the cortex that is the source of this epilepsy, is often successful in abating seizure activity, with few postoperative complications.

When neurologists assessed H.M.'s neural activity, they observed electrical storms—seizures—originating in both his left and right anterior-medial temporal lobes. As a result, William Scoville, a neurosurgeon at Hartford Hospital in Connecticut, removed the anterior-medial portion of both of his temporal lobes, including his hippocampus. Unfortunately, after the surgery, H.M. had a profound episodic memory disorder, called amnesia. If he met someone new, and then was momentarily distracted, he could not recall even meeting this person. In the morning, he could not remember what he had for dinner the previous evening. However, some of H.M.'s knowledge, or semantic memories, did remain intact. For example, he did not forget how to talk or understand other people, and he could still read, write, and perform calculations.

Through studies involving many patients, Brenda Milner, a pioneer in the field of neuropsychology and episodic memory, discovered the specific cause of H.M.'s episodic memory disorder: the removal of his inferior medial temporal lobe and especially a structure called the hippocampus (Figure 1.5). In attempting to treat H.M.'s epilepsy as best as he could, Scoville removed the parts of H.M.'s brain that were necessary for storing new memories of who, what, and where. The hippocampus is part of a network called the Papez circuit (Figure 2.2). Damage to several other parts of this network also can cause disorders of episodic memory.

Normally, people also develop other forms of memory, including procedural memories that give rise to motor skills, such as learning to ride a bicycle, tie shoelaces, or even hold a pencil for writing. Was H.M. able to learn such new procedures?

Suzanne Corkin, a Professor of Behavioral Neuroscience at MIT, worked closely with H.M. for a number of years. During one particular period, he was

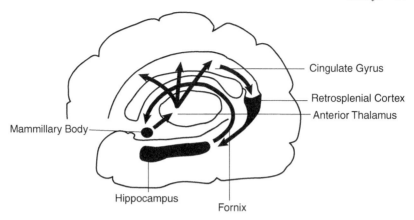

*Figure 2.2* The Papez circuit, composed of the hippocampus, the fornix, the mammil-
lary bodies, the mammillo-thalamic tract, the thalamus, the cingulate gyrus,
and the retrosplenial cortex, which projects back to the hippocampus. Damage to almost all portions of this circuit causes a loss of the ability to form
episodic memories (when, with whom, and where).

brought to her lab for a daily routine that involved learning to perform a simple,
unchanging task. H.M. was asked to keep the tip of a wand on a small target on
a rotating turntable. Just like someone with an uninjured brain, H.M. improved
with each new series of trials; indeed, he displayed the ability to learn and
remember this new motor skill.

Although Corkin spent numerous hours meeting with and testing H.M.,
he never could remember who she was. Further, from day to day he could
not recall her instructions, which were always the same and which had to be
given to him again in each new session. But somehow he managed to form the
procedural memory—the motor skills—that allowed him to perform this task
skillfully.

This study allowed Corkin and her colleagues to demonstrate something
quite vital about learning such a skill. It uses a neural network distinct from
that which is involved with remembering episodes. From research with patients
who have Parkinson's disease, neuroscientists now know that a part of the brain
called the basal ganglia (Figure 2.3a and 2.3b) are critical for learning new
procedural skills; if they are damaged or dysfunctional, that ability is impaired.
The basal ganglia have strong connections with a part of the brain in humans
called the frontal lobes, as well as the premotor and motor cortex—the regions
of the cerebral cortex involved with moving our body. This basal ganglia–
frontal network appears to be important in forming and storing our procedural
memories; H.M.'s surgery had not damaged these areas.

In a manner remarkably similar to that of finches, humans seem to do better when they acquire certain skills before puberty. Of course, as we mentioned, H.M. was certainly able to learn a new skill as an adult. But activities
such riding a bicycle, swimming, and other kinds of sports are best learned in

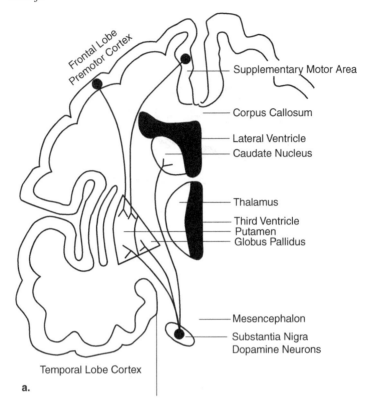

Frontal Lobe
Premotor Cortex

Supplementary Motor Area

Corpus Callosum

Lateral Ventricle
Caudate Nucleus

Thalamus

Third Ventricle
Putamen
Globus Pallidus

Mesencephalon

Substantia Nigra
Dopamine Neurons

Temporal Lobe Cortex

a.

*Figure 2.3* The premotor (frontal)-basal ganglia–thalamic–frontal network, which is important in how we acquire procedural memories.

Figure 2.3a demonstrates how information is supplied to the basal ganglia (putamen) from the premotor cortex in the frontal lobe, including the lateral premotor cortex and the medial premotor cortex known as the supplementary motor cortex. The motor basal ganglia include the putamen and the globus pallidus. The basal ganglia also receive dopamine from neurons in the substantia nigra which is found in the mesencephalon or midbrain. In this drawing, the neuron cell bodies are shown as black dots. The lines connecting the dots, the axons, and the open V or Y at the end, are the synapses that meet the other neurons.

childhood. Ken's golf game is good example of this. He did not begin playing until the age of 55, and it is still rare that he shoots less than 100 when he plays on par 72 golf courses. (If you are not a golfer, just know that that is not so good.) As with learning to ride a bicycle or ski, if Ken had learned to play golf at an early age, even after years of not golfing, he likely would have maintained a nice swing and played a better game.

Certain procedural memories can be formed over the course of a religious upbringing. Knowing the proper posture when praying or entering a place of worship, bowing the head, or making the sign of the cross—all arise from

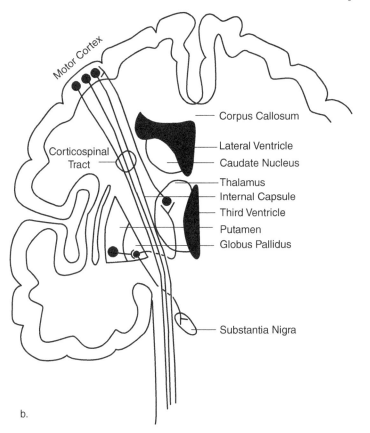

*Figure 2.3* (Continued)

Figure 2.3b demonstrates the output from the motor basal ganglia putamen to the globus pallidus, from the globus pallidus to the thalamus, and from the thalamus back to the motor cortex. It also shows how the motor cortex sends down axons to the spinal cord. The axons that excite the motor neurons in the spinal cord form a cable called the corticospinal tract.

acquired motor-skill know-how. Still other aspects of religious belief involve our capacity to learn and store things that are more informational in nature. Such semantic memories enable us to recall sacred writings, for example the story of Muhammad's time alone in the cave, the story of the birth of Jesus, or the story of Moses and the plagues.

## Making a Memorable Perception

Humans acquire semantic memory capacity differently from procedural and episodic memories. Although all memories are stored via alterations in connectivity between neurons, it is the profusion of neurons in the cerebral cortex with high interconnectivity that houses our semantic knowledge.

As we have seen, the major functions of the brain are carried out by neurons (Figure 2.4). Most neurons have many short branches called dendrites and a single longer branch called the axon. Within the cerebral cortex, the dendrites of multiple neurons connect with each other. Whereas dendrites travel short distances to meet other neurons, axons traverse longer distances and meet with other neurons; some axons bridging the left and right sides of the brain via routes through the corpus callosum. Our brain ability to function and store memories depends on this connectivity. Researchers estimate that the

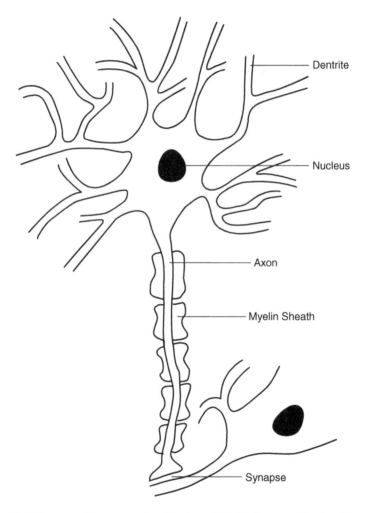

*Figure 2.4* Diagram of a neuron, showing the cell body, the axon, the dendrites, and a synapse.

number of links between neurons may be an astounding 1,000,000,000,000,000 (a thousand trillion).

The remarkable nature of our neurons is not limited to the sheer number of the connections among them. The way they function is equally extraordinary. As we have mentioned, an inactive neuron, like a battery, develops a resting electrical potential. When it fires, this resting-state potential discharges, and an electric current shoots down the axon as well as through the dendrites. When these charged messages arrive at the end of an axon or dendrite, they prompt the release of a chemical neurotransmitter. That neurotransmitter can jump across a gap, called the synapse, to neighboring neurons and activate them. In turn, these newly excited cells are themselves now able to discharge, continuing the current flow. In other cases, neurotransmitters can inhibit neurons: instead of passing on the signal, the neurotransmitters stop it.

The ability of many of the neurons in the brain to excite or inhibit another neuron is neither fixed at birth nor at any other time during life. The strength of neural connectivity can change. When two or more neurons fire together on a frequent basis, the strength of their connectivity increases. This means that when the brain responds to a particular stimulus, the neurons that are activated will tend to be activated together again, perhaps even when only part of the stimulus is repeated. In other words, our thoughts get "tied" together. Discovered in 1949 by the famous Canadian neurophysiologist Donald Hebb, this phenomenon is aptly described as *neurons that fire together wire together*. This malleable relationship between nerve cells in the cerebral cortex is the basis of how we create our semantic memories.

The brain receives memory-making stimuli through specialized receptors, for example the eye's retina, which responds to light stimuli. Other receptors include the ear's cochlea and the skin, which respond to auditory and tactile signals, respectively. These receptors ultimately convert sensory information into electrochemical signals that then are transmitted to the thalamus, a major relay station deep in the brain. From here, the sensory messages are routed to the primary sensory *receiving area* for each type of stimulus in the cerebral cortex (Figure 2.5).

These cortical sensory receiving areas begin to analyze the stimuli. The visual part of the cortex, for example, evaluates an electrochemical light stimulus for its color, intensity, location, and shape. But the analysis is not over yet. The partially processed information for each stimulus is directed to specific areas within the sensory *association cortex* for sight, hearing, and touch. Here, a convergence of the different aspects of the sensory input (Figure 2.6) takes place—and it is here that a percept—a sensory memory—begins to materialize.

How does it work? Think about the following thing. This thing is quite familiar to us, but this thing is described from the perspective of the different portion of the association cortex that deals with sight. For example, in our field of vision is a hand-sized, longish, thin cylinder, pointed on one end, blunt on the other. It is yellow, except for its pointed end, which starts as beige and ends

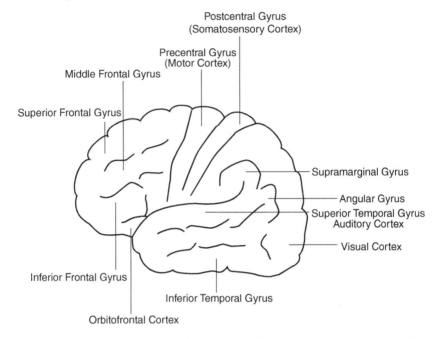

*Figure 2.5* A lateral view of the left hemisphere. The cerebral cortex has mountains and valleys. The mountains are called "gyri" and the valleys "sulci." This figure illustrates some of the major gyri that can be seen on the side of the left hemisphere. Visual information is transmitted to the calcarine, or visual, cortex; auditory information comes into the superior temporal gyrus; and somatosensory information is routed to the postcentral gyrus.

in a black tip. By looking at this object, we form an initial sensory "percept," and this percept can arouse a sensory memory of a similar object we have seen. In other words, the connections between those neurons coding for shape and those coding for color will grow more potent until a firm visual perception, something that can be recollected, is formed in the mind.

But what is this thing? Simply forming a visual precept does not inform us about what something is, or its purpose. The sensory stimuli must yet be further processed, which will happen in the cerebral cortex's temporoparietal *polymodal association* area (Figure 2.6).

This polymodal association area receives dendrites and axons from neurons in the different sensory association cortex areas in one or both hemispheres of the brain. While the polymodal area is receiving visual information about a thin yellow cylinder, it may also be getting messages from touch and articulating-joint-position association areas. In this case, what might that message be? We find that the cylinder is best positioned between the thumb and the forefinger and middle fingers; when we hold the cylinder in this position, we move the fingers, wrist, and arm. Moreover, when we combine all this information with information from the auditory association cortex (which stores previously

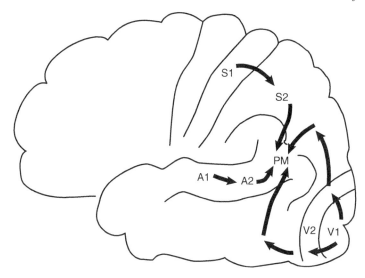

*Figure 2.6* A lateral view of the left hemisphere demonstrating the primary sensory areas. The primary visual cortex is labeled V1, the primary auditory cortex is labeled A1, and the primary somatosensory cortex is labeled S1. Each primary sensory cortical receiving area sends information only to its modality-specific sensory association area, V2, A2, and S2, respectively. All these modality-specific sensory areas send information to polymodal areas (PM) located in region of the supramarginal and angular gyri of the inferior parietal lobe.

heard speech sounds), the brain can identify the memory percept. By now, you may know that we have been talking about a typical pencil. With additional information about how the pencil enables us to express our thoughts on paper, we create a semantic memory—stored knowledge about the usefulness of pencils.

The polymodal association cortex allows any number of cross-modal associations. Think about how we seem intuitively to combine auditory and visual symbols in language. Take the letter *D* as an example. As children, we will repeatedly look at that letter and simultaneously hear its sound—the phoneme—over and over. Normally, in fairly short order, we learn that there is an association between the viewed symbol and that sound. With the neurons in our visual area that fire when they see the letter *D*, those neurons in our auditory area storing the corresponding *D* phoneme likewise will fire. Because these neurons are firing together, they will wire together—meaning that, when we have made this association enough times, we automatically will associate this visual symbol with its sound, and conversely, the sound with the symbol.

By *wire together*, Hebb meant that connectivity between these systems is bolstered, as in our example with the letter *D*. But in addition to cementing this neural association, the brain also creates an *inhibitory effect*: the visual symbol *D* will be less likely to activate neurons that represent other phonemes, even those as similar as *T*. Conversely, when we hear other phonemes, neurons associated with the symbol *D* likely will not activate.

In a similar fashion, if a child sees a dog and hears her parent say, "Dog," her mind will link the perception of the phonemic sounds *d*, *o*, and *g* with this friendly, hairy creature that barks and wags its tail. The youthful mind has an extraordinary capacity to learn, in part, related to the young brain's ability to firmly link neurons that are simultaneously stimulated. Children fire and wire together and form semantic memories exceedingly well.

During the Vietnam War, when Ken was in his late twenties, he joined the Air Force. For a time, he was stationed in Izmir, Turkey, at the NATO Hospital. Although far from family and friends, he was looking forward to something. It seems that Ken had always wanted to be fluent in another language, and he saw this deployment as an opportunity to learn Turkish. Being the good student, he studied Turkish every evening in his room. Eventually, over the course of a year, Ken was able to do something fairly simple—he could ask the grocery clerk for the things he needed. But still not sufficiently proficient in the new language, he often resorted to pointing at things and simply saying "Bu," which in Turkish means "this." He also tried to engage in conversation, but too often he could neither understand the people who were speaking nor express himself adequately.

Ken's experience probably is no surprise to most of us. However, there is more to the story. Going back a bit, a few months after he arrived in Turkey, an American tobacco merchant moved to Izmir with his wife and two children, ages 7 and 9. The kids, who could speak only English on arrival, began to interact and play with the Turkish youngsters living in the same apartment building. In a matter of several months, those darned American kids were speaking fluent Turkish, while Ken was still shopping by pointing and saying "Bu"! So malleable is a child's brain that in few months these youngsters were making auditory-visual associations that an adult brain could only partially learn in a full year. This same neural plasticity also enhances a child's ability to recover after a brain injury. For example, if a 55-year-old has a stroke that destroys his entire speech area in the left hemisphere of his brain, he will have serious trouble talking and comprehending other people's speech. On the other hand, if an 8-year-old has the same type of brain injury, we can expect to hear him speaking normally as well as comprehending other people's speech within a few months.

This recovery in the youthful brain is possible because its neurons can more readily adapt and make new, functional connections with other neurons. It is surprising that even areas of the child's brain that do not normally mediate speech can somehow learn to store the information necessary for speaking and comprehending speech. For example, Dana Boatman, a Professor of Neurology and Otolaryngology at the Johns Hopkins School of Medicine, reported on a group of children who were surgically treated for uncontrollable seizures. In these cases, the seizures appeared after the youngsters had already developed their basic language skills. Immediately after removal of their left hemisphere, these unfortunate kids had difficulty speaking and understanding words. But approximately one year later, thanks to their very malleable brains, they had regained their speech and language abilities.

Beyond this capacity for firing and wiring together, the neuronal connectivity that takes place in childhood remains very strong throughout life. This strength is evident when we consider what happen when we age, and the mind begins to deteriorate with a dementing disease such as Alzheimer's.

The brains of those afflicted with Alzheimer's disease essentially have sick neurons. Deteriorating neurons lose their axons and dendrites; as this happens, their critical ability to communicate deteriorates. Without this communication, memories, unfortunately, are lost.

In most patients with Alzheimer's, the first part of the brain to deteriorate is the anterior medial temporal lobes, including the hippocampus—the same region that was surgically removed in the patient H.M.—and one of the first signs of Alzheimer's is the inability to form new memories. Also common is difficulty with remembering names and coming up with the right words for normal conversation. Early in the course of the disease, patients usually can recall subjects they learned about as children, but at the same time, they cannot remember the stuff of later life.

It seems that many of the memories we acquire at an early age have the strongest connections in the brain. Think about that. So well preserved are the rituals, rites, prayers, religious mores, and beliefs we learn at the beginning of our lives that, even in the presence of aging and a disease as serious as Alzheimer's, these memories often persist.

Clergy and highly religious parents will diligently enforce a religious upbringing with youngsters. Almost all religions require that children start religious education at an early age. Those young people develop indelible procedural and semantic memories. They become imprinted and often remain faithful to their religion until their death and—perhaps, according to some, even after that.

# 3   More than Me

## How We Sense and Feel Beyond Ourselves

*But whoever has this world's goods, and sees his brother in need, and shuts up
his heart from him, how does the love of God abide in him?*

—1 John 3:17

### Understanding the Intentions of Others

Brooke, aged five, and her big sister Ashton, aged seven, often accompany their
mother to the health club. The girls get dropped off in the special babysitting
room, leaving Mom free to work out. Each brings her own little toy box that
holds a favorite doll and other goodies. Little Brooke's box happens to be pink;
Ashton's, on the other hand, is a very fashionable chartreuse.

On one particular occasion, Brooke goes to the restroom before opening
her toy box. While she is away, Ashton, feeling a bit mischievous, removes
Brooke's doll and hides it in her own chartreuse toy box. She then quickly
closes both containers. Now, when Brooke finally comes back into the room
and wants to play with her doll, where does she go to get it—her own toy box
or Ashton's?

Hearing this story, older children and most normal adults will report that, of
course, Brooke will think that her doll is in her own toy box, right where she
left it. However, many youngsters younger than eight will answer differently.
They will say that Brooke will go straight to her sister's toy box. Adults with
autism will often provide that same answer—that Brooke will look in Ashton's
toy box.

Kids under age 8, in general, and people with autism, know where the doll is
currently located, but they have difficulty seeing the situation through the eyes
of another person. In this case, even though Brooke is out of the room when
Aston hides her doll, they simply cannot grasp the fact that Brooke is unaware
of her sister's shenanigans.

Researchers, including Simon Baron-Cohen, the director of the University of
Cambridge's Autism Research Centre, have confirmed that people diagnosed
with autism typically are incapable of forming normal social relationships.
Many of them have some form of delayed development, often an impairment in

communicating and understanding other people's feelings. For example, some may have difficulty interpreting sarcasm, facial expressions, and the emotions expressed through alterations in the rhythm, stress, and intonation of speech.

As you might expect, not being able to recognize nonverbally expressed emotion can be detrimental to forming and keeping close relationships. Having a meaningful connection with others involves somehow understanding what they may be thinking or feeling, even when they are expressing themselves with few, or no, words. Unlike Brooke, Ashton, and other normal kids, autistic children do not play make-believe with their toys; in order to do that, they have to comprehend how or what another person would be thinking. They have to ask themselves, "How would I behave if I were them?"

Some 30 years ago, the behavioral investigators David Premack and Guy Woodruff published a famous study that delved into our innate capacity to know what other people might be thinking. Calling it the "theory of mind," or "ToM" for short, they explained that normal people have intentions. Often we can determine such intent by carefully observing another's actions; based on such observations, we can figure out what another person is thinking and feeling—or at least we think we can.

How exactly do our minds do this? We are not entirely sure. The brain networks that enable us to reason in this way—to think how another person might think—are not fully understood. There is, however, a related theory of particular significance. It centers on the concept of *mirror neurons*.

## Mirror, Mirror

Ken occasionally lectures budding neurologists and neuropsychologists. When the subject is motor knowledge and how it is stored in the brain (in other words, our memories about how we move our bodies during skilled or complex actions), he will often ask his audience a simple question: "When you remove a screw from the wall, do you make clockwise or counterclockwise movements of your arm and hand?" Then, Ken asks if they answered this problem by simply verbally knowing this information, or by visualizing a hand holding a screwdriver and removing a screw—or if they actually, covertly rotated their hands.

In a typical response, about half of the audience members will say they use visual imagery; in their mind's eye, they see a hand holding a screwdriver and removing a screw. The rest admit that they covertly moved their hands. This split response illuminates an interesting distinction in how we store and engage motor skill knowledge.

We can amass such information using sensory memories—for example, by recalling how something looked when we were doing it. Or we can develop related neural programs (think of a computer program) that enable us to perform a given function; we can then discreetly activate them as needed. When a person moves in a certain way, say by turning the hand, they receive sensory information from the involved parts of the musculoskeletal system. This information creates a kinesthetic, or movement, memory. Many of Ken's students likely were using such sensory memories when they furtively turned their hands.

In 1996, Giacomo Rizzolatti and his colleagues at the University of Parma in Italy wanted to learn how the brain recognizes another person's movements. Inserting electrodes into the brains of macaque monkeys, they recorded neural activity while the monkeys performed two slightly different activities. During one, the monkeys grasped an object using a motion not unlike that imagined by Ken's students; in the other, they simply watched another monkey perform a similar action. In the seconds before the activity, when the monkeys were planning the movement, their premotor areas, located in front of the motor cortex (Figure 3.1), showed an increase in activity. This happened before the motor cortex itself showed similar engagement. Why should this be?

Neurons in the motor cortex extend all the way down to the spinal cord, where they connect with lower motor neurons. The lower motor neurons often are bundled together as motor nerves that go to specific muscles (Figure 3.2). When a neuron in the motor cortex fires, it transmits electrical signals down its axon to the spinal cord. These signals excite the lower motor neurons, which discharge and send their message to the motor nerve and muscle; this causes the muscle to contract and move a given part of the body.

When a particular part of the motor cortex is stimulated, a corresponding joint will move. For example, if the region in the lower portion of the motor

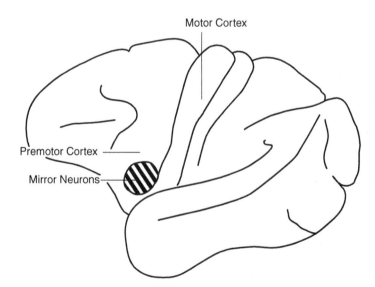

*Figure 3.1* Diagram of a monkey's left hemisphere, illustrating the motor cortex and the premotor cortex. The mirror neurons that Rizzolatti and colleagues described are located in the ventral aspect of the premotor cortex.

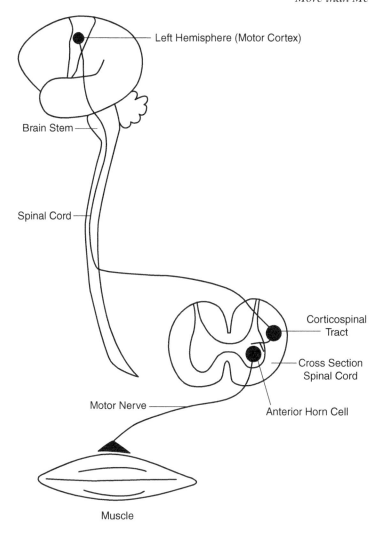

Left Hemisphere (Motor Cortex)

Brain Stem

Spinal Cord

Corticospinal Tract

Cross Section Spinal Cord

Motor Nerve

Anterior Horn Cell

Muscle

*Figure 3.2* Lateral view of the left hemisphere, showing the primary motor cortex. The motor cortex sends axons to the motor neurons in the spinal cord. The motor neurons in the spinal cord motor send their axons into the motor nerves, which travel to the muscles. When these lower motor neurons fire, a message is sent down the motor nerves that are connected to muscles. This activation makes these muscles contract. These contractions enable the body to move.

cortex is stimulated, it might cause the thumb on the opposite side of the body to twitch; if we stimulate a higher position, the wrist will flex.

The premotor cortex, located in the frontal lobes directly in front of the motor cortex, contains neurons that carry information to the motor cortex.

Unlike with the motor cortex, stimulating the premotor cortex might cause, for example, the entire arm to make a complex movement. This is because it activates whole systems of motor neurons. It appears that the premotor cortex contains neural movement "programs" that, like blueprints, determine the overall form or framework of an intended action.

Rizzolatti discovered that when a monkey watched one of his neighbors make a meaningful motion or action, the lower portion of the premotor cortex became active *in the observing monkey*. At other times, when monkeys intentionally made copycat motions, those same premotor neurons fired. So these neurons linked the memories of observed actions with intentional, physical self-actions—they were mirroring that which they observed.

If we are watching someone else's behavior, could our own mirror neurons help us understand his or her intentions? In essence, do we automatically "mind read" by covertly mirroring other peoples' actions and then asking ourselves what would lead us to behave this way?

Dimitrios Kapogiannis, a neurologist at the National Institutes of Health, along with his coworkers, published a study in which 40 individuals were asked to respond to statements about their religious beliefs. For example, they were queried about how intimate was their relationship with God or if they experienced a fear of God. During this process, the researchers measured the volunteers' brain activity using fMRI. When the researchers posed questions regarding God's intentions, they found something intriguing. The activated brain networks in the study participants were very similar to those observed in people under functional imaging when they were attempting to understand the intentions of others. An especially busy area, the inferior frontal lobe (Figure 2.5), happens to be the counterpart to the premotor area in the monkeys' brains—the area containing mirror neurons.

Rizzolatti's research showed that the macaques' premotor neurons were activated when they watched and mirrored the movement of other monkeys. But in Kapogiannis's study, there were no movements to observe. Why were his participants activating the mirror-neuron region of the brain? Were they imagining what the actions of God might be, and then somehow mirroring them to "know" divine intention?

### Who Did It?

The idea of ToM requires someone to cause something to happen. The resulting event, something as simple as a facial expression or as complex as a series of behaviors, can reveal the person's intention. The person who created or caused the event is referred to as the agent.

We are not strangers to the concept of agents because it is supported by how we construct and use language. An easy phrase to understand, the commonly used declarative sentence, would say something like, "Ashton moved the doll." According to some linguistic theories, when people hear a complex sentence that initially may be unclear, they mentally convert it into one or more simple, declarative sentences. For example, when we hear the passive sentence, "The doll that was in the pink box and is now in the chartreuse one was moved by Ashton," our language networks may translate this into "Ashton moved the doll from the pink to the chartreuse box."

Simple, declarative sentences usually have the agent (in this case, Ashton) as their first word; the agent has the intention and causes something to happen. The verb *moved* describes the action, and the object or patient (the doll), at the end of the sentence, is the recipient of this action. When someone sees Ashton move the doll, or hears the sentence, "Ashton moved the doll," they will most often assume that Ashton's intention was to put the doll in another place. Normally, people, it seems, will consciously or unconsciously assign intentions to almost all actions.

A 2003 study by Justin Barrett of Oxford University and Amanda Johnson of Calvin College showed that people seem compelled to believe in intent. Barrett and Johnson showed healthy subjects geometric figures, such as circles and squares, moving randomly around a computer screen and then asked them what they were seeing. The common response was, "figures chasing one another," for example. The subjects regarded some of these objects as symbols of agents with the intention of catching the other objects who were the patients.

If we are compelled to react this way, does such agent detection offer some benefit? The theory of evolution suggests that many of the brain's functions evolved and remained unchanged because they provided us with a survival advantage. Certainly, humans, like other animals, have had to deal continuously with marauding predators and enemies. Failing to detect that kind of danger is risky and even deadly. Indeed, it is better to be safe than sorry. According to Barrett and Johnson, this bias leads us to be hypersensitive to agent detection.

The neural networks that mediate ToM require an agent. But when events occur that seem to have no apparent cause, what do our minds tend to do? Barrett and Johnson proposed that, when we see or experience events where there is no obvious agent, our hypersensitive agent-detection system might try to come up with one. Many of life's events occur with no apparent agent. Without even being aware of it, do we tend to fill that agent position with a supernatural power?

During the Middle Ages, many people believed that the Black Death—the bubonic plague—was God's punishment for their sins. Some even flagellated themselves, hoping to be forgiven and spared from the plague. Today, of course, we know what the agent is a bacteria that is carried by fleas. If someone should develop signs of plague infection, proper medical attention, rather than self-flagellation and asking God for forgiveness, is the preferred treatment. The history of almost all religions tells of altars and temples, where animal and even human sacrifices took place, as well as of acts of repentance such as fasting, prayer, and even self-flagellation. All these things are a part of worship, but perhaps they are also a way of seeking approval from or appeasing some divine entity. After all, appeasement somehow may satiate or assuage an agent's predatory drive. Are acts of appeasement the result of a hyperactive agent-detection system? Perhaps. Then again, maybe this whole discussion is merely an indicator that the authors of this book need to seek an explanation—an agent—for something that is, in the end, inexplicable.

## What's Up and What's Down? What's In Here or Out There?

### *Spatial Metaphor*

Ken and his colleagues, Paul S. Foster, Valeria Drago, Greg Crucian, and others, conducted a study in which they asked twenty normal individuals to think about a number of different emotional experiences from their past. They were to recall events involving surprise, happiness, humor, disgust, anger, and sadness, and lastly, a neutral experience. After they recollected each type of memory, the subjects were instructed to use a pen to make a mark anywhere they wanted on a large sheet of paper. When recalling emotional memories, people will often remember who, when, and where, the details of the episodic memory. However, they are also likely to re-experience some of the feelings associated with the event. With that in mind, Ken and his colleagues discovered that, in general, the placement of marks associated with positive emotional experiences were located *above* those associated with the negative memories.

There could be a couple of reasons for these results. One may have something to do with what is known as *spatial metaphor*. Throughout our lives we learn that certain words express meaningful concepts because of the sense of space they portray: this is a *big* idea; he's a *small* thinker; or she is *deep* thinker. Think about how someone might express the emotional feelings mentioned in this study. For happiness, maybe they would recall happy sentiments of feeling *up* or *elevated*. Contrast this with sadness where a person might remember feeling *low* or *down*. Even the word *depression* means to push down.

We seem to employ spatial metaphor naturally, don't we? Perhaps it is entirely arbitrary, or maybe it is related to some environmental or biological factor. After sundown, in the dark of the night, humans, unlike other animals with highly developed senses for nighttime foraging, are more vulnerable to danger. For early humans, the bright light of daytime was the anticipated salvation from the darkness. Is this why words such as *brightness*, *light*, and *up* are related to the divine—and why *darkness*, *down*, and *below* are sometimes metaphors for evil?

One way to determine whether such spatial expressions are more than arbitrary is to look for uniformity among different cultures and languages. Remember that in Chapter 1, we mentioned that Paul Ekman showed that people from a large variety of cultures (including some that were relatively isolated) used similar facial expressions for a range of emotions, such as sadness, anger, surprise, happiness, disgust, and fear. Those investigators found that, although the words used to describe feelings were often composed of different speech sounds, people universally recognize such facial expressions.

This universal recognition suggests that these facial expressions are more than arbitrary gestures—they appear to be genetically coded.

Unfortunately, unlike with Ekman's work with the universality of facial expressions, we do not know of similar investigations into the kind of spatial metaphor we are writing about here. We have learned, however, that expressing sadness by using spatial metaphors such as "I am feeling low or down or depressed" is something that a number of languages have in common with English. The same holds true, of course, for terms such as *up*, *high*, and *elated*, which convey the emotion of happiness.

Given this cross-cultural use of vertically oriented, up-or-down spatial terminology, it is possible that distinct portions of the brain are engaged similarly in all humans, independent of their culture or language. It is possible that when different neural networks are activated, we associate emotions with some sort of spatial frame of reference. What does all that mean? Let's take a closer look, because it may play a role in how we think about heaven and hell.

Many animals have one or more keen senses, such as sight, smell, or hearing, that allow them to locate things are in the environment. Although humans also employ these senses, our primary means of locating objects in space is our vision. As the process of sight begins, light enters the eyes, streaming through the lens to the retina at the back of the eye. Stimulated by the incoming light, the retina sends electrochemical information through the optic nerves and their branches, the optic tracts, to the optic thalamus, a relay station deep in the core of the brain. These coded electrochemical signals containing messages about the spatial organization of the light's intensity and color. Ultimately, the optic thalamus relays this information to the back part of the cerebral cortex, the occipital lobe, where the primary visual cortex is located (Figure 3.3). This primary visual receiving area in the occipital lobe (or the calcarine cortex) helps determine the spatial patterns and configuration of what we are seeing.

Next, visual information from these occipital receiving areas is passed to regions in the cerebral cortex called visual association areas (Figure 2.6). These networks, located in more forward regions of the occipital lobe, as well as the adjacent temporal and parietal lobes, perform further analyses of the incoming visual information.

When we look straight ahead at an object, the portion of the object that is above eye level will be projected back to the bottom of the retina (Figure 3.4). The portion of the object below eye level is projected to the top part of the retina. As mentioned, this information is sent to the primary visual cortex in the occipital lobe. The information above eye level goes to the bottom (ventral) portion of the occipital cortex, and the information from below the eye to the top (dorsal) portion of the occipital cortex.

From the occipital lobes, this information is further processed by two major *visual association networks*—one network is in the higher (dorsal) portion of the occipital and parietal lobes, and the other network is in the lower (ventral) portion of the occipital and temporal and lobes. And our inherent use of spatial

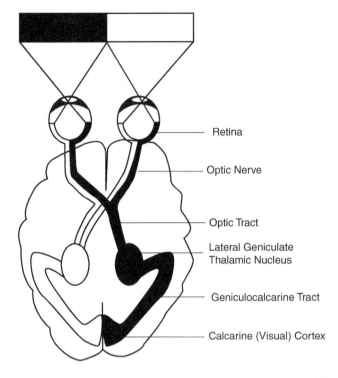

*Figure 3.3* The visual system. When looking straight ahead, stimuli on the left side goes
the right half of each retina in the back of the eye; stimuli on the right side
go to the left side of each retina. The retinas send this visual information to
other areas of the brain via the right and left optic nerves. The visual information that comes into the right side of the left eye's retina is carried by the
optic nerve and crosses from the left to the right half of the brain. Stimuli that
fall on the left side of the right eye's retina also cross. The fibers from the left
half of the retina in the left eye and the right half of the retina in the right eye
do not cross. On each side of the brain, these fibers converge at a relay station
in the thalamus (lateral geniculate nucleus) and then travel from the optic
thalamus to the primary visual cortex in the occipital lobes. Thus, each hemisphere's visual cortex receives information from the opposite visual field.

metaphor—for a heaven above and a hell below—may arise from this *higher-
dorsal* versus *lower-ventral* dichotomy.

The late-nineteenth-century German neurologist Heinrich Lissauer first
reported that people with an injured *ventral visual association* network could
see and locate objects in their environment, but they could not recognize them.
Nor could they describe where such objects might normally be found or how
they might be used. This disorder, called visual *agnosia* (from Greek, "without
knowledge"), can have some unusual symptoms.

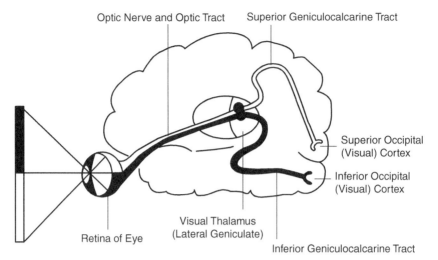

Optic Nerve and Optic Tract    Superior Geniculocalcarine Tract

Superior Occipital
(Visual) Cortex

Inferior Occipital
(Visual) Cortex

Retina of Eye

Visual Thalamus
(Lateral Geniculate)

Inferior Geniculocalcarine Tract

*Figure 3.4* Vertical (above and below eye level) visual streams. When we look straight ahead and something appears in our vision above eye level, the image of this object is projected into the bottom of the retina. An object below eye level is projected to the top part of the retina. Once the retina detects this information, it is sent to the brain by the optic nerves and tracts until it reaches the thalamic relay station. From the thalamus, the information travels to the primary visual cortex. The information above eye level goes to the bottom (ventral) portion of the occipital cortex, and the information from below the eye to the top (dorsal) portion of the occipital cortex.

Several years ago, a very worried wife brought her 72-year-old husband to the emergency room because the couple thought that he was suddenly going blind. It seems that after Hank had awakened that morning, he could not recognize anything on the breakfast table. However, he could see where objects were located and could reach for and feel them with his hands; once he felt them, he knew what they were.

The emergency-room doctors suspected a stroke. Immediately after performing their exam, they requested a neurologist. Ken got the call, quickly proceeded to Hank's bedside, and began by testing his vision. He asked Hank to try reading a newspaper that had been left in the room. Hank could not do it. That suggested to Ken that Hank was suffering from impaired visual acuity or maybe alexia, the loss of the ability to read.

Ken next scribbled a small dot on a piece of paper and asked Hank to touch the spot. Hank could do it, and quite accurately at that—pretty good evidence that his trouble with reading the newspaper was not due to a loss of visual acuity. The exam continued. Ken held up a set of keys and asked Hank what they were. "I can see what you are holding," Hank replied, "but I don't know what it is."

"Can you tell me what you do with these things?" Ken continued. Hank had no idea. Then Ken rattled the keys, and suddenly Hank responded, "Sounds like keys." Continuing with similar questions, Ken eventually tried this: he pointed to his own nose and asked Hank to continue looking at it without moving his eyes; then, as Ken placed his hand about 12 inches below Hank's eye level, he asked him if he could see Ken moving his finger. He could. Ken slowly raised his hand. When it reached Hank's eye level, Hank exclaimed that it was gone! He could no longer see it. In fact, Hank could not see Ken's hand at any point above his eye level.

Later, talking with the emergency-room doctors, Ken shared his diagnosis: a likely stroke to the bottom of Hank's occipital and temporal lobes. He explained that injury to the *lower-ventral* visual association area would cause problems seeing things above eye level and would impair his ability to read and recognize objects. A subsequent MRI scan confirmed Ken's diagnosis.

In contrast to Hank with his visual object agnosia, some patients have lesions of the dorsal visual system. The Hungarian physician Rezso Balint reported that these patients, unlike those described by Lissauer's with visual agnosia, were able to recognize objects; however, if asked to take an object from the examiner's hand, they had trouble doing so. They would move their eyes to incorrect spatial positions and could not visually locate and focus on the target except through trial and error. But even while gazing right at the object, they would still then move their hands to incorrect positions. Only through more trial and error of hand and eye movements could they eventually take hold of the object.

A surprising paradox is that although moving their eyes and hands to focus on and touch objects in front of them was challenging, when these patients were blindfolded, each had no difficulty finding his or her own outstretched hand with the other hand. This observation indicates that they did not have a hand or arm motor-control problem. In addition, they showed no impairment in other types of sensation involving, for example, the position of a finger or elbow joint. All of this evidence indicates that the problem is predominantly in these patients' visual systems.

The ventral visual network, necessary for the visual recognition of objects (visual object agnosia)—described by Lissauer—is referred to by Leslie Ungerleider and Mort Mishkin, who are at the National Institutes of Health, as the *what* system. The dorsal visual network, important in determining the location of visually sensed objects, is called the *where* system [Figure 3.5]. When people interact with an object in the environment, they need to know what the object is, as well as its location in relation to their bodies. But this is not all. Beyond these *what* and *where* systems, several other key, spatial perceptions merit a closer look.

### What's Up and What's Down

It turns out that we have a sophisticated physiological system for sensing an object's position in relation to our eyes, our head, and our body. When we view something located on the left side of our field of vision, its image will project

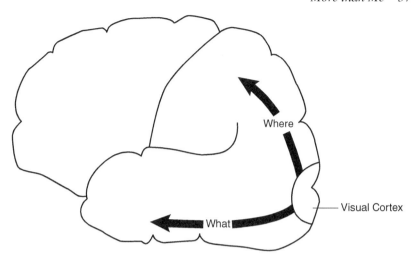

*Figure 3.5* The two visual streams. After the primary visual cortex analyzes visual stimuli, they undergo further analysis in visual association areas. One set of visual association areas are in the lower or ventral part of the occipital and temporal lobes. This network is important for the perception and recognition of objects. In this drawing, this ventral network is called the "what," stream. The other set of visual areas are in the higher or more dorsal part of the occipital lobe and parietal lobe. This network is called the dorsal "where," stream. This visual association network is important in determining the location of an object in space in relation to the body.

to the right side of our retinas. Objects on the right will project to the left side of the retinas. Things we see in the visual field below eye level will transmit to the top of the retinas; those above, to the lower portion (Figures 3.3, 3.4, 3.5).

Because the visual information from the left side of space is sent to the right occipital lobe, and stimuli on the right side of space are sent to the left occipital lobe, if someone has an injury to the right side of the occipital lobe or the pathways leading to it, he or she will be unable to see objects on the left; the converse is also true. Something similar also occurs for our sense of vertical positioning—what is *up* and what is *down*.

### What's Out There and Right Here?

A number of years ago, Ken and his colleagues examined a patient named Hazel who had suffered from a stroke in her upper (dorsal) "where" system (in this case, the parietal lobes). Just as Balint had described, after the stroke, Hazel had difficulty figuring out where things were in space. She often moved her hand to the wrong place when trying to grasp an object. In attempting to look at something, she had trouble moving her eyes into the right position. When Hazel, who was from a rural farming area, was questioned about how the world looked different since her stroke, she replied, "Cows seem to float in the air." Asked what that meant, she replied that she no longer saw their feet. That was a phenomenon not described by Balint.

Wondering if Hazel truly was unaware of stimuli in the lower portion of visual space, Ken assessed her with something known as a line bisection test. A clipboard with a sheet of paper was held facing Hazel, straight up and down and about 15 inches from her nose. On the paper were a series of straight, vertical lines; the clipboard was positioned so that the midpoint of the lines was about at eye level. To start, Hazel was asked to bisect, or find the middle of, each line and mark it with a pencil. Next, Ken requested that she cross out certain small lines that had been randomly drawn all over a second sheet of paper. Hazel could not perform either task correctly. She placed all her line bisection marks above the midpoint of each vertical line and failed to cross out the lines drawn on the lower portion of the paper.

Her upward bias on this test and her failure to see and cross out lines on the lower portion of the page could not be explained by partial blindness, since even patients with such blindness can compensate by moving their heads and eyes. It was evident that Hazel's dorsal "where" system injury resulted in a lack of awareness of lower space.

Ken and his team were also curious about Hazel's ability to see things that were near her. She was tested again with the same clipboard, now held parallel to the floor and below her eye level. This time, though, the lines on the paper radiated out and away from her body. Hazel was asked to bisect these lines. Now she consistently misplaced her marks beyond the midpoints, farther away from herself. These results indicated that, besides deficits in her "where" system, Hazel had a specific problem attending to, or being aware of, things that were below eye level and close to her body. Let's call it a "down and in here" deficit, because it involves the space below eye level within a person's immediate environment.

In contrast to Hazel, another patient had stroke damage in his ventral "what" system. Whereas Hazel had a "down and in here" attentional deficits, this patient was impaired in detecting stimuli in upper and more distant space, an "up and out there" deficit.

### Any Conclusions?

Can we draw any conclusions from all of these phenomena? And what, if anything, do these neural networks have to do with religion? We have seen that the dorsal "where" system is body centered; it is associated with those portions of the brain that attend to space that is lower and close to us. In contrast, the ventral system is outer-object centered. It is integrated with the neural networks allocating attention to upper space and items that are farther away.

Can certain emotions or moods disproportionately engage these systems? Think about feelings such as sadness, hopelessness, and depression. Might these emotions somehow be more connected with the "in here" system, which centers on the self and directs our attention in and downward? And what about joy, happiness, elation, and feelings of success? Could these emotions be closely aligned with the "out there" system, which moves our attention away from ourselves, up and outward toward other people and things?

We know that if people avoid a period of grieving after the loss of a loved one, they can experience a chronic, detrimental change of mood. Jewish tradition includes a formal period of mourning called "sitting shiva." After the death of a close family member, mourners remain at home for seven days with all the mirrors and pictures in the house covered. Although friends and relatives visit, traditionally the visitors do not greet the family or initiate conversation. Friends might provide food during this time, but the bereaved do not work or conduct business, shop, or cook. Nor do they groom, wear jewelry, or have sex. The grieving family sits on low stools and keeps their gaze downward.

Do these rituals, which are intended to encourage introspection and feelings of sadness, activate the dorsal "in here" system and direct attention within and down? Could looking at pictures or mirrors and interacting with visitors engage the ventral "out there" system, prompting unwarranted out and upward attention, away from the grieving self?

## Heaven's Place?

Humans have the brain physiology and function that permits spatial perspective— a sense of things being up or elevated, down or low, far or near. What about our religious beliefs? Are they a reflection of this spatial sensing capability? Or, rather, do our religious beliefs shape our perspectives?

Symbols in Western religions, such as the crucifixes in Christian churches, are almost always placed above eye level. Church steeples stretch upward to the heavens. From ancient times, monuments and structures built for worship were often placed on the highest sites. In early America, before insurance companies and banks owned the tallest buildings, the church steeple was the highest structure in a community. Inside these houses of worship, the cleric's spatial position, usually higher than the congregation's, forces the observant to look upward. The holy books tell us that heaven is up, that ascension is a divine direction, and that hell is below us. During prayer and atonement, when we look inside, we humble ourselves before God by kneeling, bowing down, or lowering our heads. We are taught to look down on sin and sinful acts but to lift up our hearts through prayer and supplication.

Is God to be beseeched as some divine entity in a heaven up or out there somewhere? Are we merely lowly humans, down here and separate from what is above? We cannot say. One thing is fairly certain: most likely the "out there" brain system would be engaged during thoughts about an external divinity in a place called heaven. Likewise, our "in here" system is active when we assume an inward or lowered perspective.

The existence of a God in heaven somewhere out there is the core belief of the world's three great monotheistic traditions: Judaism, Christianity, and Islam. What about the more mystical aspects of these religions, as well as of Hinduism, the world's third-most populous religion? Most of humans' experiences are dependent on sensory input, but those that are mystical are not. These experiences come from within. Instead of a heaven that is only an "out there" experience, the sense of the self—the "in here" part—is allowed to expand to encompass, and join with, the "out there." "In here" and "out there" are sensed as a heavenly unity. Might this mean that those regions of the brain that mediate "in here" and "out there" are simultaneously engaged? We do not know. But in the pages to follow, we investigate some intriguing possibilities— starting with a look at the left and right hemispheres of the brain, and how each may play a distinctly different role in our religious and spiritual habits.

# 4    Left Brain, Right Brain

## Religious, Spiritual . . . and More

*I form the light and create darkness. I make peace and create evil. I the Lord do all these things.*

—Isaiah 45:7

## Seeking the Cause

It goes without saying that the more we know about the cause of any given event, the better our chance of improving our well-being and, in some cases, our chances of survival. Once we learn that thunderstorms can produce dangerous lightning, it makes good sense to take cover before the ominous dark clouds arrive. When we experience indigestion, it is important to know the food culprit (or restaurant!) so we can avoid it in the future. We may notice someone behaving in a peculiar way. If we suspect that such actions could lead to a dangerous situation, we get away from that person. Although we are often unaware of it, our brain seems naturally programmed to search for and understand cause as a means of anticipating outcomes.

Curious about this seeming need to seek a cause, John Yellott, an Associate Professor of Psychology at the University of Minnesota, undertook a creative and important experiment. He arranged for normal subjects to sit facing two lights, one on the left and the other on the right. The subjects were told that either light would flash on; sometimes it would be the left, sometimes the right. The lights were programmed so that the flashes would occur on a particular side 80 percent of the time, with the remainder on the other side. The order in which the light flashes switched from side to side was randomized. At the start, participants were asked to try to predict which light would go on. Although they were told that the light on one side would flash more often than the other, they were not informed about the random programming.

Yellott found that participants' predictions were influenced by how often a light flashed on a given side. If the left light flashed 80 percent of the time, participants predicted more often that the left light would, indeed, come on. Of course, if they consistently predicted that the left light would come on, they would have been correct 80 percent of the time. However, because they saw that sometimes the light on the other (right) side flashed (it did, randomly, 20 percent of the time), they occasionally guessed that it would. Although on rare occasions they were correct when they predicted that the light on the other side would flash; overall, making these guesses reduced their percent of correct predictions to less than 80 percent.

Yellott reasoned that on occasion, people would predict the less common side because they were attempting to learn the lighting pattern. With that in mind, he changed the programming for the last set of tests. Now, when a participant guessed which side would light up, the prediction, unknown to the participant, caused that side to, in fact, light up.

When the experiment concluded some fifty trials later, Yellott asked the participants how they made their predictions. There was a pattern, the majority said, and by the end of test, they had figured out what it was.

Seeking a pattern—the cause behind lights flashing on one side or the other—seems like a natural maneuver, and one we employ automatically in order to predict a future outcome. Yellott's experiment suggests that even when presented with simple information in a game-like setting, we try to find some pattern or meaning; we try to connect the dots. And although the rodents fared better in predicting future occurrences, the lower-scoring humans were attempting to learn a pattern, to find some connection between the occurring disorder and what might happen in the future. Is that meaningful?

The pull toward finding a thread that joins seemingly unrelated things (such as the flashing lights), and to arrive at some new, orderly outcome is the very basis of creativity. It has enabled humanity's advances throughout the ages and the profound enhancement of our well-being. Think of the uncanny—and invaluable—associations discovered between the mold and bacterial infections; electricity and the human voice; and even energy and matter. We are talking, of course, about the antibiotic penicillin, the telephone, and the dawn of the nuclear age.

What do we do when meaningful events occur with no apparent cause? It seems that we naturally insist on the existence of patterns to explain even such inexplicable events. Does this innate compulsion—a drive that often keeps us from danger and has aided our survival as a species—also lead us to believe in an all-powerful, all-knowing, supernatural being who enforces his will, requires obedience, and bestows blessings or punishes?

## Left-Brain Logic

In 1868, the French physician and anthropologist Paul Broca reported that when right-handed people lost their ability to speak as a result of a stroke, the damage most likely occurred in the brain's left hemisphere. Later studies also showed that many of our mental functions are mediated primarily by either our left or right hemisphere, affectionately referred to as the left and right brains. As we saw in Chapter 3, when we look straight ahead, a visual stimulus on our left results in a transmission of signals to our right brain; one on the right to our left brain (Figure 3.3). Likewise, each hand is controlled by the opposite side of the brain.

Remember that the main crossroads for communication between the left and right brains is the corpus callosum (Figure 1.2). It allows each hemisphere to share certain kinds of memories and stored knowledge with the opposite hemisphere. In patients with epilepsy, a seizure can start in one hemisphere and spread to the other. Recall that although many of these patients can be successfully treated with antiepileptic medication, those who cannot might elect to have their corpus callosum surgically severed in order to control the spread of seizures from one hemisphere to the other.

Studying patients who had the corpus callosum surgically divided gives researchers a wonderful opportunity to see how each side of the brain stores different kinds of knowledge and mediates particular behaviors. Think about this: each hemisphere acts independently because it has been surgically divided from the other. Because we can easily present a patient with a stimulus on one side or the other, we can be certain about which side of the brain is receiving and mediating each response. If a visual stimulus is shown on the patient's right side (right half of the visual field) it will be processed by the brain's left hemisphere; similarly, if he touches something with his right hand, only his left hemisphere will process the sensation. Conversely, when a patient with a callosal disconnection sees something on her left side (left half of the visual field) or touches something with her left hand, this sensory information will be processed by the right hemisphere. Studying split-brain patients allows us a glimpse into how each hemisphere seeks meaningful patterns and relationships.

Michael Gazzaniga is a Professor of Psychology at the University of California, Santa Barbara, and the director of the SAGE Center for the Study of the Mind. Curious about which hemisphere drives us to seek and understand the cause behind events, he set up a study using participants who had had the corpus callosum surgically divided. Using a prediction method similar to Yellott's, he asked his research participants to sit in front of a computer monitor. They were instructed to watch the screen for a left- or right-pointing arrow that would indicate on which side of the monitor (left or right) a light would next appear. They were also told that the light could appear in the upper or lower portion of each side of the screen. Additionally, when the directional arrow pointed to the left, they were to use the left hand to respond, and vice versa. Finally, once an arrow pointed to a side of the screen, the participants were asked to predict whether the upper or lower light would appear on that side; they did so by pressing one of two buttons with the left or right hand as dictated by the arrow's direction.

As you might realize by now, since each participant's corpus callosum had been severed, the responding hand received instructions from only one half of the brain. The actions of this hand reflected the cognitive process of the hemisphere on the opposite side—the left hand from the right brain, the right hand from the left brain.

The study was designed so that the participants used their left and right hands an equal number of times. And although the order in which a top or bottom light appeared was randomized, one appeared significantly more frequently than the other, as in Yellott's study. What happened?

Gazzaniga found that the right brain consistently predicted that the more frequently appearing light would be the one that would, again, come on. Just as Yellott's animals unfailingly went to the same side for food, each human subject's right brain apparently did not attempt to find any pattern and instead went with the flow of information. In stark contrast, the left brain worked to analyze and find meaningful patterns—and its predictions were less accurate.

Gazzaniga performed another study that he reported in the *Scientific American* in 1998. In this study, a split-brain patient was shown an image in her right visual field—in this case, a picture of a chicken. At the same time, a second picture (a wintry snow scene) was displayed in her left visual field. The subject then was shown an array of other pictures and asked to point successively with one hand, and then the other, to the pictures that were associated most closely with the two original images. Her right hand, controlled by her left hemisphere (the same side of the brain that received the image of the chicken), pointed to a chicken's foot. In contrast, her left hand, controlled by the right hemisphere (which received the image of the wintry snow scene), pointed to a snow shovel. Good so far, right? Well, when the subject was asked to explain her choices, she responded, "It's simple. The chicken foot goes with the chicken, and you need a shovel to clean out the chicken shed." But why did she respond in this manner?

The right brain has a limited ability to express thoughts through speech. With the corpus callosum severed, the subject's right hemisphere—which had received the visual snow scene stimulus and then prompted her to point to the snow shovel picture—could not have access to the left brain's memory or to its logic and speech areas. Her right hemisphere could not articulate the reason that her left hand, controlled by the right hemisphere, pointed to the snow shovel. Because the left hemisphere, which programs speech, had no information about the right hemisphere's processing of a snow scene, it could not provide in words a reason for her choice. In addition, because the left hemisphere is the deductive, calculating, and analytical side of the brain, it seeks causal relationships; without access to the right hemisphere's snow-scene memory, the verbal left hemisphere sought a cause for the left hand's pointing to a shovel. Working with the image in its memory—the chicken—the left brain tried to associate the shovel and the chicken.

As we go about our lives, we may very well be employing deductive reasoning, even if we are unaware that we are looking for causal relationships and patterns. In thinking about a problem in this manner, we draw conclusions that are based on certain understandings. The conclusion is true or valid if the prior understandings are true, for example, "All people are mortal. Because Jim is a person, he is mortal."

In 2005, the neuroscientist Nicola Canessa, a research fellow at the University Vita-Salute San Raffaele in Milan, Italy, and colleagues performed a functional imaging study of normal subjects that seems to support the two Gazzaniga studies we have just discussed. When participants used deductive reasoning to search for logical relationships between a conclusion and those things on which the conclusion was based, the left brain was the primary region of neural activity. Religious leaders and interpreters of religious texts frequently rely on deductive reasoning and the writings of Thomas Aquinas (1224–1274) are a choice example of such deductive logic.

A product of an influential Italian family, St. Thomas Aquinas joined the Dominican order when he was 20 years old. Combating heresy was important work for the Dominicans, and the order stressed the value of education, girding themselves with knowledge. During the thirteenth century, learned scholars in Paris studied the classical Greek philosophers, such as Plato and Aristotle. Dominican monks immersed themselves in the use of logical proofs and deductive reasoning to support their beliefs. In his famous *Summa theologiae*, St. Thomas Aquinas used deductive reasoning to structure his Five Proofs of the existence of God.

The First Proof is based on the principles of physics. St. Thomas Aquinas recognized that movement is intrinsic to the things of the earth and that force underlies these many different movements. Every moving thing, then, must be forced into movement by something else. In turn, this something else had to be moved by another something else. Following this logic, he concluded that at the origin of this process would be a primary, or first, mover—God.

The Second Proof, similar to the first, deals more directly with causation: there cannot be an infinite chain of causes and effects; some original thing was uncaused, and this is God.

The Third Proof deals with contingency. Things that are contingent are not omnipresent. If everything were contingent, there would have been a time when nothing existed. But if the universe was empty at some time, it would have remained empty; therefore, nothing would exist. Because we do indeed exist, there has to be a thing that is not contingent; that non-contingent being is God.

St. Thomas Aquinas's Fourth Proof states that everything has properties. Some objects have more of these properties and others have less. Therefore, there should be an entity that contains all the properties, and this is God.

The Fifth Proof deals with goals. Every object has a purpose, a reason for being. Whereas some objects have minds, others do not. These latter, mindless objects had to be created by a being that has a mind; that being is God.

Our lives are replete with different experiences. Many of us quietly long to know why certain things happen, but much goes explained. Perhaps our left brain, which relies on logical justifications, will find causes that may involve supernatural phenomena. The logic behind St. Thomas Aquinas's proofs is a stark portrayal of the left hemisphere's capacity to form calculated, yet, as we can see, quite simplistic beliefs.

There is some evidence, however, that left-hemispheric-mediated analytic and deductive reasoning may not enhance religious beliefs. In 1998, Edward J. Larson and Larry Witham reported the results of a questionnaire that inquired about religiosity, belief in God, and heaven that they sent to 517 members of the United States National Academy of Sciences (NAS). Larson and Witham reported that belief in God and in immortality among NAS biological scientists was very low. For example, the biological scientists had the lowest rate of belief (5.5 percent in God, 7.1 percent in immortality), with physicists and astronomers only slightly higher (7.5 percent in God, 7.5 percent in immortality).

To learn how analytic thinking effects religious beliefs, in 2012 Gervais and Norenzayan published a paper in *Science* that provided evidence that when people engage in analytical thinking, they are less likely to have strong religious beliefs. Scientists are trained to think analytically. The results of this study indicate that perhaps analytical thinking leads to high rates of atheism and agnosticism. Since the left hemisphere primarily mediates analytic-deductive thinking, perhaps the right hemisphere plays a critical role in enabling us to believe in the divine.

## Right Brain, Global Attention, and the Theory of Mind (ToM)

Through our ability to engage in the theory of mind (ToM), we can somehow mentally place our minds, so to speak, outside ourselves and into another person's frame of mind: we can shift our emotional perspective to people and things outside of us. Does that sound like a primary left or right brain function? Can studies of patients with strokes and the use of functional imaging in normal subjects help us determine the hemisphere that primarily mediates ToM?

Whereas ToM involves the ability to shift our attention to another person's frame of mind, we should briefly explore several forms of "attention." The left brain mediates a particular ability called focal attention. The right brain, in contrast, mediates something different—global attention. The distinction between them is illuminated in studies that employ Navon figures [Figure 4.1]. A Navon figure is a large symbol, such as the letter *T*, for example, that is composed of many smaller-sized letters of the alphabet.

Looking at such a Navon figure, certain patients with hemispheric damage will report seeing the large letter, but not the smaller ones that compose the large letter. Another set of patients will say they see only the smaller letters and completely overlook the large figure in which the small ones are located.

The first group—those who saw the whole but missed the pieces—likely have normal right-brain function, but damage or dysfunction in the left brain. Conversely, the second set of patients—who readily saw the small letters and missed the big, overall symbol—likely have some form of right-brain injury. Such Navon-figure studies seem to indicate that the left hemisphere tends to pick out the component pieces, whereas the right sees the larger whole.

Tests that assess someone's capacity for ToM involve the simultaneous recognition of multiple factors. Although we do not know for certain, perhaps

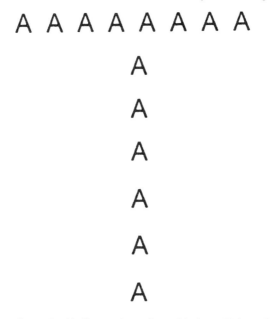

*Figure 4.1* Navon figure. In this figure a larger letter (the letter *T*) is made up of smaller *A* letters. People with a deficit of global attention (simultanagnosia) will name only the smaller *A* letters in this figure. A person with a deficit of focal attention will see only the larger *T* in this figure.

ToM depends, at least in part, on global attention. In functional imaging studies, people carrying out tasks that required ToM showed increased activity in their right hemispheres. In an extensive study, Richard Griffin and coworkers at the Tufts University Center for Cognitive Studies found that ToM deficits were associated with right-hemisphere strokes. In addition, some patients with the most severe ToM deficits had lesions in a part of their right brain that is analogous to the mirror-neuron area in Rizzolatti's monkeys.

An interesting question arises from these observations. If people has an injury to their right brain in the region of these mirror neurons, such that they can no longer "mind read" by covertly mirroring other people's actions, would they also cease believing in the same God? In other words, if their God was reflection of their own human attributes—one with similar thoughts, feelings, and intention—would their God's nature now be radically changed?

## Prayers, Music, and the Things We Know by Heart

Halévy Shapiro was born and raised in Paris; he was 82 years old when Ken first met him. During the Second World War, like many other young French Jewish men not killed or forced into labor and concentration camps, Halévy fought with the French underground. In spite of France's Nazi-collaborating Vichy government, he simply loved France and continued to live there in the postwar years. He was, however, an Orthodox Jew, and at every table-side Pass-over service, he would repeat the words, "Next year in Jerusalem." Although to many Jews this expression is a wish for the Messianic era, the Orthodox believe in the literal interpretation. Truth be told, Halévy longed to live in Jerusalem before he died, and he did; when he was 80, he and his wife, Molly, moved from Paris to a small apartment in Jerusalem.

Since he was a boy, Halévy, like most Orthodox Jews, would chant the short monotheist prayer, often called the Schma, several times a day. The person praying says, "Schma Israel, Adenoi elohenu, Adenoi echad" (Hear oh Israel, the Lord is our God, the Lord is One). It is a simple prayer, but after waking up one morning in their apartment, Halévy attempted to recite this prayer, but he could not. Of course concerned, he went into the kitchen, telling Molly, "I think I might have had a stroke. I am having trouble talking." Listening to him, she replied that he was speaking just fine but suggested they get to the hospital.

Ken was a visiting professor at Hebrew University in Jerusalem when Halévy arrived for evaluation by two of Ken's former fellows, Lynn Speedie and Eli Wertman. An examination showed that Halévy's spontaneous speech seemed normal. He was able to read, write, understand, and repeat speech, and name objects. Psychiatric disease was ruled out, and his general and neurological examinations were entirely normal—except for one thing: when asked to say some of his prayers, he could not do it.

Strokes of the left brain's frontal lobe often result in difficulty with fluency and trouble with speaking spontaneously, known as Broca's aphasia. Such patients often make speech-sound errors and have difficulty naming objects and even repeating words they are hearing from others. Although these patients find it challenging to communicate their thoughts and ideas (propositional speech), they often have relatively well-preserved automatic speech. They can say things they know by heart: they can count, recite the alphabet, name the days of the week. Often they can sing well-known songs and even recite their prayers.

The observation that patients with left-brain injury often have preserved automatic speech suggests that, unlike propositional speech, which appears to be mediated by the left hemisphere, automatic speech might be primarily mediated by the right hemisphere. Because Halévy lost the ability to pray, which is often a form of automatic speech, but still had the ability to carry on a conversation, maybe a stroke had damaged the frontal lobe in his right brain.

To see if this was the case, Ken and his colleagues asked Halévy to say some simple things he should know by heart, like counting and saying the days of the week. Halévy could not do it. They asked him what songs he liked to sing and he replied *La Marseillaise*, the French national anthem, and the *Hatikva*, Israel's national anthem. But when asked to sing them, again he could not do it. Subsequent brain imaging showed that, indeed, Halévy had suffered a stroke in his right frontal lobe (Figure 4.2).

Halévy's condition is not an isolated case. Ken and his coworkers have seen a number of similar patients. Some have had strokes, others degenerative diseases that caused a loss of neurons in the right frontal lobe. The finding that

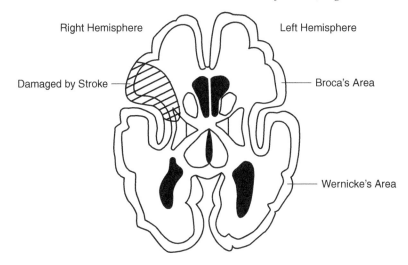

*Figure 4.2* Drawing of the areas affected by Halélvy Shapiro's stroke, showing damage to the right frontal lobe and basal ganglia. After having this stroke, Halévy was unable to say his prayers or sing songs that he had known since his childhood.

injury to the right frontal lobe causes the loss of these abilities suggests that, when a normal, healthy person recites a deeply ingrained prayer or chant or sings such a song, the right frontal lobe is mediating this activity.

In 2003, Keith Jeffries and his research colleagues at the Voice, Speech and Language Branch of the National Institute on Deafness and Other Communication Disorders used PET imaging to determine what parts of the brain become active when uninjured people speak, and then when they sing a familiar song. They found that, while the subjects were speaking, portions of the left hemisphere showed increased activation. In contrast, during singing, the researchers observed relative increases in activity in portions of the right brain. Other investigators have reported similar outcomes.

Music, as we know, is often used to express and share emotional feelings. In 1722, the French composer Jean-Philippe Rameau wrote about such feelings and musical harmony in a revolutionary work, the *Treatise on Harmony*. The major mode, Rameau said, is most suitable for music that expresses mirth, joy, grandeur, or magnificence. Conversely, minor chords convey something different, perhaps tenderness, sadness, or mourning. Undoubtedly his writings are not so revolutionary today. We have become accustomed to major and minors chords evoking those respective feelings.

We do not know why music is so evocative of feelings. Certainly, we can and do convey emotion by altering the stress and intonation patterns of our speech. Prosody, as it is called, arises from changes in speech pitch, timbre, loudness, and the rate at which words are spoken. A hundred years ago the famous British neurologist John Hughlings Jackson noted that patients whose left hemisphere was damaged through stroke or other diseases often lost their ability to carry on a normal conversation. (Recall that in Chapter 1 we talked about this basic propositional form of speech.) He noted, however, that they were able to communicate emotion using such prosody.

Studies by Ken and his co-investigators at the University of Florida's College of Medicine (1984) and by Elliot Ross (1993) at the University of Oklahoma confirmed Hughlings Jackson's suspicions and have provided evidence that, unlike the conversational, propositional speech mediated by the left brain, emotional prosody appears to be most influenced by the right brain.

Audibly expressing our sentiments is, of course, not unique to humans. Our four-legged friends communicate their feelings through their vocalizations. Psychologist and Professor of Informatics Norman Cook of Kansai University, and his colleague Takefumi Hayashi reported in 2008 that animal vocalizations with a descending pitch communicate strength and dominance; those with an ascending pitch, submission. They pointed out that even humans have very basic, universal emotional responses to different musical chords; these arise, perhaps, from some instinctive understanding of sound frequencies.

With its alterations in tone, timbre, amplitude, and timing, music has much in common with the emotion prosody of speech. Brenda Milner has performed a number of studies of patients with epilepsy, including one involving music. She assessed patients by testing their musical abilities both before and after a procedure to surgically remove the offending portion of the brain, the seizure locus. Milner found that when people had the temporal lobe of their right hemisphere removed, they lost their ability to recognize melody and timbre. Taking out the temporal lobe in the left hemisphere did not alter these skills. Additional research on stroke victims and other people with hemispheric injuries suggests the same.

Beautiful music, hymns, and chants play a significant role in much of our worship, and it is no wonder that they do. Music can trigger loving feelings of submission to God's power and majesty, and more, perhaps even euphoria. But there may be another reason that activation of the right hemisphere may enhance our feelings of closeness to God.

We have all had or at least heard about déjà-vu experiences—that we previously have seen a particular place or experienced a particular event. Certain people with epilepsy can have the opposite experience. At times, in their own homes, for example, they may feel as if their surroundings are entirely new. The seizures that cause these *jamais vu* experiences commonly start in the right brain's temporal lobe.

Reports of some hospitalized patients with brain injury give us some insight into a different kind of familiarity problem. Visited by close family, such as his wife, for instance, a patient recognized her face and her voice, but afterward he would tell his nurse or doctor, "That person looked and sounded exactly like my wife, but it wasn't really her." This disorder, too, is most commonly seen with right-brain injury. Its cause is a bit of a mystery. One theory suggests that, normally, when we see someone we know, emotional feelings and memories arise, whether we are consciously aware of them or not. But these patients do not experience the emotions normally induced by seeing close family. It seems that their right-brain injury results in communication disconnection: the posterior (back) portion of the ventral (bottom) part of the temporal lobe and the ventral portion of the occipital lobe, in an area called the fusiform gyrus, which is important for facial recognition (Figure 4.3). With injury to the right hemisphere that disconnects this fusiform gyrus from the areas in the anterior temporal lobe, these stored memories of previously seen faces becomes disconnected from those areas vital to feeling emotions.

In a way that is similar to our ability to recognize faces, we can also distinguish familiar voices. Injury to the posterior (back) superior (top) region of the temporal lobe, called Wernicke's area, can result in the inability to understand words (Figure 4.4). Patients with this injury cannot comprehend speech because the portion of the brain that normally stores the sound memories of previously heard words has been damaged.

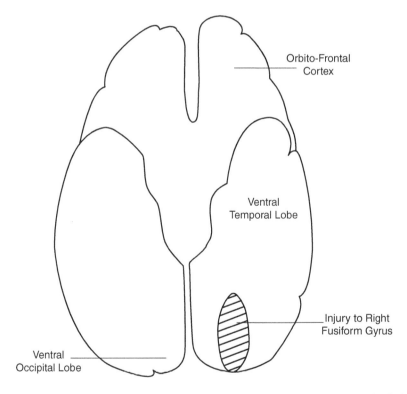

*Figure 4.3* Drawing of the ventral (bottom) portion of the brain demonstrating the fusiform gyrus of the right hemisphere. When this area is damaged by a stroke, patients cannot recognize faces of people that they know but can recognize those people's voices.

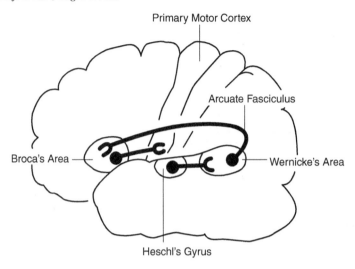

*Figure 4.4* The language cortex. Diagram of the left hemisphere demonstrating the major areas important in speech, including Heschl's gyrus, the primary auditory area that performs analyses of the incoming sounds; Wernicke's area, which is located in the posterior portion of the superior temporal gyrus and contain the memories of the speech sounds or phonemes of previous learned words; the arcuate fasciculus, which connects Wernicke's area to Broca's area and carries information between these areas; and Broca's area (pars opercularis and triangularis), which programs the motor movements needed to make the speech sounds.

Although such patients cannot understand words, they can recognize the voice of the person speaking to them. In contrast, an injury to the same part of the brain in the right hemisphere can produce a disorder in which individuals recognize spoken words but not the voices of those speaking to them. It seems that if this damaged area in the right brain is still intact but has lost its neural connection with other areas important for emotional experiences, the patient will be able to recognize the voice—but will not have the emotional memories that goes along with the sound of that voice. We would hear comments such as, "That sounds like my wife's voice, but it is not really her."

Does something similar happen during worship services? On hearing the voice of a beloved minister, priest, or rabbi, do we spontaneously feel positive emotions? Do religious hymns, repeatedly heard since childhood, engender warm feelings? It would seem so.

## Got to Have it

There may be another reason why music is an important part of worship. In the 1930s, the famous behavioral psychologist B. F. Skinner developed what psychologists refer to as the Skinner box. Animals (or people) placed inside are exposed to different stimuli, such as red and green lights, and can press specially designed levers to obtain rewards of food or drink. If a green light comes on, for example, and the animal presses a lever, it gets a food reward. But if it presses the lever when it sees a red light, there will be no reward. Skinner and other behavioral psychologists noted that when a behavior was rewarded, the subject would continue to perform the behavior. In contrast, if a behavior was not rewarded, the animal would stop doing it.

In an important study dating back to 1954, James Olds and Peter Milner of McGill University inserted electrodes into a variety of locations inside the brains of lab rats, and then placed them in a Skinner box. Whenever the animals pushed a lever, an electric current would be sent through a given electrode to activate the brain tissue immediately surrounding it. The researchers noticed that when the rats pressed a lever stimulating a region deep in their brain near the nucleus accumbens (Figure 4.5), something quite interesting happened. They continued pressing the lever without obtaining a food or drink reward. In fact, the desire to press the lever and receive an electrical stimulus was so strong that even when hungry and thirsty and presented with food and water, the rats chose pressing the lever over eating and drinking.

We are not entirely sure why a stimulated nucleus accumbens compels more of the behavior that stimulates it. This nucleus receives input from several different areas in the brain as a part of an anatomically distributed circuit known as the ventral striatum. This ventral striatum receives input from the ventromedial (lower middle) portion of the frontal lobes. The frontal lobes appear to be

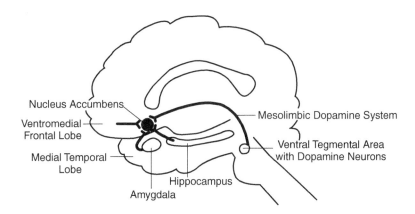

*Figure 4.5* Diagram of the nucleus accumbens. Activation of this nucleus is associated with reward. This diagram also shows the other portions of the brain that connect with this nucleus, including the ventromedial frontal lobe, the hippocampus, the amygdala, and the mesolimbic dopamine system from the ventral tegmental area of the midbrain (mesencephalon). The output from the nucleus accumbens (not shown in this figure) travels to the bottom (ventral) part of the basal ganglia.

critical in allowing people to performing behaviors known as "executive func-tions," including the ability to conduct what the famous Russian neurologist Alexaner Luria called goal-oriented behavior. Such behaviors include antici-pating future conditions, preparing for them, and performing actions that will enable people to gain what they and their loved ones need or should possess.

A second source of input to the nucleus accumbens is the olfactory tuber-cle, which delivers information about stimulating aromas and fragrances, as well as repulsive odors. Another, the mesolimbic dopamine system (Figure 4.5 and Figure 4.6) in the midbrain, gives off the neurotransmitter dopamine, which activates the nucleus accumbens. By means of an extensive network, the nucleus accumbens sends neurons deep into the brain to the ventral palli-dum, and from there to the thalamus, which is strongly connected to the frontal lobes. It is the activation of this network that gives rise to the pleasure and satisfaction of reward.

Because the frontal lobes mediate our capacity for long-term planning and activate the motor system to pursue our goals, this neural network might be acting as a feedback loop: when we achieve a goal, the executive system gets

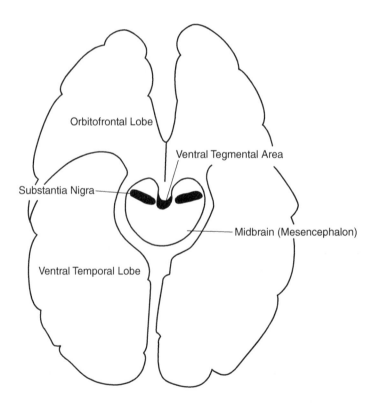

*Figure 4.6* The ventral tegmental area of the midbrain. This area contains neurons that make dopamine and send this dopamine by a pathway called the mesolimbic system to the nucleus accumbens.

positive feedback. It is not surprising that the nucleus accumbens, together with input from the dopaminergic system, is activated by drugs that are commonly abused, such as cocaine, opium, and morphine. In some respects, addicts are similar to the lab rats that continually pressed the "reward" lever for the electrical activation of the nucleus accumbens.

Karl Marx did not know about the nucleus accumbens. Nor did he know about the effect of opium on this reward system. But he did say, "Religion is the opium of the masses."

Does song play some role in connection to religion? We have already mentioned that Keith Jeffries and his colleagues reported the results of a brain-imaging study that they performed to learn about what happens in the brain when people sing. Using positron emission tomography (PET), in addition to finding that the right hemisphere activates during singing these researchers observed increased blood flow in the nucleus accumbens, a part of the reward network, of their singing participants. This would suggest that singing, like opium and cocaine, might activate the reward network and perhaps induce a form of addiction.

In another study, Vinod Menon of Stanford University's School of Medicine, together with Daniel J. Levitin of McGill University, also reported that listening to music strongly increases activity in the reward-processing network, including the nucleus accumbens.

Although Ken does not sing while he plays golf, every once in a while he will hit a few good shots; the memory of those seems to be enough of a reward to bring him back another weekend for more. It is a little like gambling: someone can win or lose money, but occasional random wins can (and often do) reinforce gambling behavior. Indeed, behavioral psychologists have demonstrated that behaviors that are randomly reinforced and rewarded tend to persist. Is that what compels so many people to prayer?

Some prayers are answered. But occasionally having a prayer fulfilled may be a form of random reinforcement and could very well activate the nucleus accumbens network. For many, religious activities are very rewarding. In some cases, people make significant sacrifices in order to adhere to their religious beliefs. Perhaps, throughout such devotion, the nucleus accumbens is receiving its reward.

# 5  Suspending Disbelief
## The Ability to Believe

*Immediately the father of the child cried out and said, "I believe; help my unbelief!"*

—Mark 9:24

## Going to the Movies

How many times have we been immersed in a book or movie that becomes so real that we cry or are frightened or even sick to our stomachs? Later, of course, we realize that we became emotionally engaged in an illusion. If you think about that, it is quite an odd behavior for animals as intelligent and modern as us. After all, the characters on the screen—3D or otherwise—are played by paid actors (whom we have probably seen in other performances). If we are reading words on some paper pages or a flat Kindle, it is even more of a stretch!

So why do we emotionally respond to these fabrications? We know that normally, people have an immediate physical response to sudden, disruptive stimuli. For example, when we hear a loud, unexpected noise, we will spontaneously blink our eyes and tense our muscles. That behavior is not without purpose, though, because the blinking protects our eyes and the increased muscle tension prepares us for fight or flight. Called the startle reflex, this reaction is controlled by the brain stem, the most primitive part of the brain. However, the cerebral cortex and limbic system, which allow us to comprehend and experience emotion, also appear to influence this reflex. Let's say we are relaxed, in a good mood, and watching a wonderful comedy; suddenly we hear a great big bang. Certainly we would be startled. Now think about our reaction to the same noise if we are completely engaged in a nail-bitingly scary, suspenseful movie. We might jump out of our seats. Different reactions such as these suggest that, in some way, the mind is treating these movies as more real than not.

Our willingness to behave as if some work of fiction is true, even if it is fantastic or impossible, is what the British poet and philosopher Samuel Taylor Coleridge called the "suspension of disbelief." In other words, we immerse ourselves in a make-believe world for the duration of a book or movie (although some fans of the movie *Avatar* seemed to continue believing beyond the movie). Have you noticed, though, that not everyone does this?

Many people relish going to movies to experience the story. Other viewers seem unmoved. Some people suspend their disbelief in some situations but not in others. Why this happens is a bit of a mystery. Recall that Giacomo Rizzolatti found that neurons became active in the monkeys' premotor cortex when they observed another monkey moving (in a meaningful way). We also know that sometimes when we see the expression on somebody's face, or even if we just read a vivid description of an expression, we mimic it. Maybe the mirror-neuron systems important in culturing empathy also play a role in our immersion in a story line.

Age and our brain's maturity somehow influence our willingness or ability to suspend disbelief. In his college days, Ken had great fun working at a kids' summer camp. On some dark, star-filled evenings after supper, the camp director would call all the excited little campers to the campfire to roast marshmallows, sing songs, and listen to Ken and the other counselors tell stories. As it happened, Ken was asked to share these stories with the older children, mostly 12- to 14-year-olds. Now, one of his favorites was W. W. Jacobs's spooky tale "The Monkey's Paw."

The story goes like this: a British military man returns from India with a preserved monkey paw that apparently has special powers. The fellow leaves the creepy thing with a family he knows, telling them that it will grant three wishes to whomever holds the paw. It seems that the family is not wealthy, so they wish for a good sum of money. In a horrible accident, when their son goes to work the next day, a machine collapses and crushes him to death. The company where the accident occurred compensates the family with a sum of money that just happens to be the same amount for which they had wished. Anyway, the son is buried; his mother and father miss him terribly, so using the monkey's paw again, they wish for their son to come back to them. He does, but returning from the grave, the boy is mutilated beyond identification and putrefying, a horrible sight. Of course, Ken added ample gory detail to his story telling.

Well, the older kids just loved it, and when the other counselors heard about the fun, they asked Ken to share "The Monkey's Paw" with their group of 8- to 10-year-olds. Naturally, he obliged them at the very next campfire. The youngsters seemed attentive, as if they were enjoying the story, but the next day, Ken learned of their real reaction: many were upset and had trouble falling asleep. Worse, some pleaded to call their parents so they could go home! Ken felt terrible about all this, but he puzzled over the difference in the children's reactions. The older kids suspend disbelief just during the time they were listening the story. Once the story was over they no longer suspended disbelief. They were well aware the story was fictional. But why would the younger ones who also suspended their disbelief not let it go after to story was over? Why did they persist at their suspension of disbelief?

This kind of thing happens so often that we probably take it for granted. Think about how many children's TV shows we have seen over the years that, by design, are farcical and intended for young, open-minded kids.

Our ability to hold on to and to let go of beliefs seems to arise primarily from interactions between the more posterior temporal and parietal lobes of the cerebral cortex and the anterior frontal lobes, which are strongly connected to each other. The region in the back (posterior) of the brain receives and interprets sensory information and helps us approach and engage things. Conversely, the frontal lobes enable us to move away and disengage. The noted neurologist Derek Denny Brown, who was Chairperson of the Harvard Neurological Unit, along with Richard Chambers, proposed that these two regions work like a teeter-totter: when one is more active, the other is less so.

The frontal lobes in both the left and right hemispheres in young children are not yet fully developed; in fact, they are the last part of the brain to mature fully. Recall what we said in Chapter 4 about the left brain's involvement with logical justifications. Well, maybe a youngster's ability to suspend disbelief for sustained periods, even for the most far-out stories and myths, is related to the relative immaturity of their frontal lobes. Perhaps it is this particular delay in development that allows religion to be so readily imprinted on young children. Kids are more likely to accept biblical stories as being literally true. Many leaders of fundamentalist groups realize that starting religious education at an early age promises a long line of loyal believers: "Train up a child the way he should go; and when he is old, he will not depart from it" (Proverbs 22:6).

The neuroscientist Sam Harris and coworkers (2009) observed increased frontal-lobe activation when study subjects believed a religious story. The area that was activated was the ventromedial portion of the frontal lobes, and as we mentioned, this part of the brain is connected with the nucleus accumbens, which is a critical area in the ventral striatal reward network. Many religious stories and beliefs stretch the boundaries of what is plausible; perhaps so many people readily accept them because suspending disbelief and believing is strongly rewarding.

## Let's Pick and Choose Our Beliefs

Studies employing functional imaging (fMRI) and brain electroencephalography (EEG) indicate that healthy individuals have the ability to train their thoughts and deliberately activate or deactivate portions of their brain. Some people, however, can do this better than others. As adults with fully developed frontal lobes, have some of us been so conditioned from a lifetime of saying, "That's just make believe," that we simply do not fall for fictional story lines, whereas others excitedly engage them? Of course, the 3D movie *Avatar* prompted the suspension of disbelief in many people, whereas others viewed it as only a movie. What of believing Bible stories? Are some of us similarly conditioned?

As a practicing neurologist, Ken has watched how parents respond when their beloved children are stricken with serious diseases. Despite all the advances in treatment methods and fervent praying by family, church members, and friends, many beautiful, innocent children suffer and die. So many times, even after the deepest grief and pain, religious parents continue to have faith in an all-powerful, all-knowing, loving God. Somehow, perhaps these moms and dads—who have endured more than any parent should—unconsciously side with the solace found in suspending disbelief.

Rejecting Darwin's theory of evolution is commonplace among Christians today. This theory clearly contradicts some interpretations of the biblical story of creation. But think about this: some six or seven decades ago, when penicillin first became available, it was effective against almost all types of bacterial infections. However, over the years, some pathogens, such as methicillin-resistant *Staphylococcus aureus* (MRSA) have developed a high degree of resistance; the tried-and-tested antibiotics are no longer effective. If someone who refuses to accept Darwin's theory of evolution becomes infected with MRSA, what should they do? Refuse the newly developed and only effective antibiotic? It seems that accepting evolution to save one's life may be a good idea after all.

## A Reward after All?

As we mentioned before, using functional imaging, Sam Harris and his colleagues asked 30 participants to judge the truth or falsity of certain religious and nonreligious statements. Half the participants were devout Christians, and half considered themselves nonbelievers. In addition to examining other comparisons, the investigators looked at which parts of the brain became active when people believed, or did not believe, a given religious story. They found that when people did not believe—in other words—they could not suspend disbelief, their lateral frontal lobes were activated. However, when they accepted a story, the parietal-occipital region of the cortex and a different portion of the frontal lobe became engaged. Also, as mentioned, believers experienced activation of the ventromedial portion of the frontal lobes, the region connected with the nucleus accumbens, which when activated allows the emotional sensations of reward.

Should that latter finding be surprising? Immersing ourselves in a storyline, whether we are listening to a Bible story in our place of worship, watching a movie, or reading a book, is pleasurable and somehow, maybe even rewarding. Do these pleasurable feelings secretly motivate us to continue doing these things? If so, maybe we need to look at our beliefs in a somewhat different light.

# 6 The Brain Does Some Peculiar Things

## Obsessive Compulsive Disorder and Religiosity

*Take care lest you forget the Lord your God by not keeping his commandments and his rules and his statutes, which I command you today, lest, when you have eaten and are full and have built good houses and live in them, and when your herds and flocks multiply and your silver and gold is multiplied and all that you have is multiplied, then your heart be lifted up, and you forget the Lord your God.*
—Deuteronomy 8:11–18

### OCD: Obsessive and Compulsive Disorders

Obsessive compulsive personality disorder and obsessive compulsive disease, or OCPD and OCD, as we usually refer to them, are psychiatric disorders. Sigmund Freud, the famous father of psychoanalytic theory and psychotherapy, played a key role in first describing these disorders. A trained neurologist and curious about brain-behavior relationships, Freud discovered these disorders while studying patients suffering from neurological diseases.

As with so many other psychiatric illnesses, there are no visible, physical attributes or biological tests by which these two disorders can be diagnosed. So how are they assessed? Most psychiatrists rely on the behavioral criteria set forth in the *Diagnostic and Statistical Manual of Mental Disorders* (*DSM-V*), published by the American Psychiatric Association. According to the manual, many patients with OCPD are preoccupied with details, rules, lists, order, and organization; a number are overly conscientious and inflexible about ethics, morality, and values. Although the symptoms of OCPD are not terribly disabling, those with OCD do suffer and can be incapacitated by their obsessions and compulsions. For our purpose here, it is not necessary to distinguish between the two; when we use the term OCD, think of it as including both.

People with OCD have recurrent thoughts that intrude on their activities. Many times these thoughts are inappropriate and usually accompanied by anxiety. Realizing that these intrusive thoughts are not based entirely on reality, OCD sufferers will try to rid themselves of or ignore them. Many people with this disorder also have compulsions, driven by their obsessions, to perform certain behaviors. These behaviors often are repetitive and rigidly performed.

For example, a person with this disorder may repeatedly check a door to see if it is locked or will count or say certain words over and over. Sometimes the person with OCD does these things because he or she believes they may prevent some terrible and dreaded event from happening.

Freud noted that in many respects, the behaviors associated with religiosity—repeated practices and expressions of devotion to God, and strict adherence to teachings and beliefs—were similar to those he saw in patients with symptoms of OCD. This observation was supported much later in a study by Fred H. Previc at Texas A&M University, who reported a strong relationship between hyperreligiosity and OCD. But Freud also believed something else: religiosity, he said, was genetically transmitted. Moreover, it was an obsessive, compulsive neurosis, both pathological and universal in nature.

According to David L. Pauls, studies of family aggregation have suggested that OCD is familial. Results from twin studies provide further evidence that the familial nature of OCD is due in part to genetic factors. However, there is an important difference between people with OCD and those who are highly religious: unlike OCD sufferers, who often realize that many of their obsessions are delusive and not based on reality, those who are highly religious think their firmly held beliefs and actions are absolutely justified and validated by unquestionable constructs of God and God's laws.

Habitual thoughts about washing the hands or locking the door and compulsions to follow through on such thoughts are common in individuals with OCD. In a similar way, do we have persistent repeated concerns, even obsessions, about living a Godly life? Russell's grandmother, Esther, said her rosary three times a day, every day, in the morning, at noon, and before she went to bed at night. During the day, Esther's rosary was in her pocket; she would pull it out whenever she needed to bless herself or others in need. Her rosary always went under her pillow at night, along with her purse. She followed all the rules of fasting, she went to church without fail (unless she was sick), and regularly received Holy Communion. These are all beautiful habits; how much they pressed on her like an obsession, Russell cannot say.

What underlies the persistent drive that some of us have to read scripture or pray every day, attend worship services frequently, confess our sins regularly, tithe, or adhere to food restrictions or particular dress codes?

According to the Hartford Institute for Religious Research, about 118 million Americans attend worship services every Sunday and those of us who feel the need to engage in repeated religious behaviors might not be clinically classified as having OCD, although some people could have the disorder. According to research by the clinical psychologists Stanley Rachman and Padmal de Silva, the signs and symptoms of OCD occur in some 70 to 80 percent of America's population—the same percentage of people who claim to be religious. Is this more than coincidence? Perhaps. Suggesting that certain recurring religious behaviors may be associated with OCD is not an indictment of so many devout practices. However, we might give consideration to what might sometimes be the invisible motives behind them. As we have seen, people with recurring obsessive-compulsive thoughts and behaviors become anxious and worried about not following through on these intrusive inner voices. Do some of us sometimes adhere to religious edicts and teachings for similar reasons? Viewing life through a religious and morally stern looking glass keeps us constantly on guard: we must eschew what we consider "improper" thoughts and "sinful" behavior lest we face dire consequences.

Studies of religious Muslims and Christians performed by Orçun Yorulmaz at Uludag University's Department of Psychology and his co-investigators support the idea of a strong association between religiosity and OCD. Along with coworkers, Professor and Associate Chair of Psychology Jonathan Abramowitz at the University of North Carolina, Chapel Hill, looked at the relationship between Protestant religiosity and the symptoms of OCD. Dividing the study population into moderately and highly religious Protestants and atheists or agnostics, the researchers found that the highly religious group reported more severe OCD symptoms. These included compulsive hand washing and the need to control recurring unwanted, intrusive thoughts, even when the participants were not acting on them.

In the United States legal system, we are not punished for thinking about committing a crime. Much of Christianity, though, does not offer that leeway. In Christian theology, God may punish even evil thoughts. The Book of Revelations in the New Testament tells us that God knows what we are thinking. When we stand before him on Judgment Day, he will judge us not only for our actions but also for our thoughts. President Jimmy Carter, for many years a member of the Southern Baptist Church, probably read Matthew 5:28, which says, "Whosoever looks at a woman lustfully has already committed adultery." In an interview, the former president commented, "I've looked on a lot of women with lust. . . . I've committed adultery in my heart many times."

*DSM-V* notes that at some time during the course of their OCD illness, patients become aware of their recurrent thoughts and actions as intrusive and time consuming; they find their work and social functioning becoming impaired. Yet despite this awareness, they continue to engage in repetitive OCD behaviors to reduce distress or avert some dreaded event (that they fear might cause some kind of suffering or even death).

Benjamin Greenberg, an Associate Professor in the Department of Psychiatry and Human Behavior at Brown University, and Gaby Shefler at the Hebrew University of Jerusalem's Department of Psychology found that symptoms of OCD were observed in a significant number of Orthodox Jews. A number of those observed cited the codes of Jewish law to justify their compulsive behaviors. Of course, Muslims and Christians also can and do use religious law to support certain repetitive actions. But although highly religious people exhibit many of the same types of behaviors as those who are diagnosed with OCD, there is an important difference between the two groups: unlike those simply diagnosed with OCD, the religious are not concerned about excessive, repetitive thoughts and actions. Indeed, they find meaning and importance in such behaviors.

## In the Family?

Like OCD, religiosity may run in families. Behaviors that are common to members of the same family suggest that they might be inherited. Remember that earlier we discussed how the behaviors and beliefs of parents are often imprinted on their children. We know, then, that family values and practices play an important role in forming a child's understanding of life, his or her behaviors, and especially the youngster's religious beliefs.

What is inherited and what is learned? To understand better the role of genetics and imprinting—nature versus nurture—investigators will often employ something known as a concordance study. Using identical twins with the same genetic makeup (hence the term *concordance*), they look for symptoms or behaviors that occur in one twin, but not the other. When such a difference occurs, it can indicate that non-genetic or learned factors are at work. For example, if one twin develops a genetic disease, the other should as well. If a condition is fully genetic, then we should see a 100 percent concordance between the twins. This would be true, of course, whether they were raised together or not.

In contrast, without a genetic influence, the probability that both twins will contract the same disorder is no different than that for any other two people in the general population. In those cases where just one of the twins has the malady, then multiple factors, both genetic and environmental, are influencing the twins' health.

Concordance studies might be the best way to learn whether a behavior is inherited or learned, but they have a limitation: finding identical twins who have been separated since birth is often challenging, so it is hard to get a clear understanding of environmental influences.

Another kind type of concordance study involves both identical and fraternal twins. The results of this research revealed that identical twins show a higher concordance rate for OCD than do fraternal twins. This result indicates it is more likely that this behavioral disorder has a genetic aspect. Along with his colleagues, Daniel S. van Grootheest at the Department of Biologic Psychology and Department of Psychiatry of Vrje University Amsterdam examined OCD in twins. He found a moderate OCD concordance in identical twins, higher than the rate for fraternal twins or nontwin siblings. If one identical twin had OCD, there was about a 50 percent chance the other twin would also have OCD. These results suggest that OCD is caused by a combination of genetic and learned factors.

Torsten Winter and coworkers at the University of Helsinki's Department of Public Health examined religiosity in more than 4,000 Finnish twin boys and girls. They found that identical twins were more likely than fraternal twins to have the same religious practices. Like OCD, religiosity appears to be partially inherited and partially learned.

If heredity plays a role in determining who will be religious and who will not, as these twin studies suggest, some genetic factor may influence physiological brain function. Unfortunately, the brain mechanisms that give rise to

OCD are not entirely understood, but neuroscientists are at work and new discoveries are at hand. It appears that dysfunction of the most evolved part of the brain—the frontal lobes and their networks, which normally play an important role in disengagement—have a relevant and vital role.

## Influenced from Within or Without:
## The Phenomenal Frontal Lobes

A particular grouping of brain processes regulate our ability to make appropriate choices, to create and implement plans, and to exercise flexibility in our reasoning as we take those plans through to fruition. We refer to these processes as the *executive functions*. We refer to the neural networks that mediate them as the *executive system*.

The actions that we perform to ensure that we and our loved ones have adequate resources and that all are kept safe as well as provided with a home environment that supports self-actualization are considered to be the most important executive functions, according to the Russian neurologist Alexander Luria. Luria and a number of other neurologists have noted that patients with defects in the frontal-executive networks have impairments in goal-oriented behaviors. One of the first and most important reports about frontal-executive functions was John Martyn Harlow's report on Phineas Gage, published by the Massachusetts Medical Society in 1868. As a result of an explosion, a tamping iron penetrated Gage's skull, injuring both of his frontal lobes. Gage survived this horrible accident, but his personality underwent a dramatic change. Harlow's report describes a number of symptoms that we know today are forms of frontal-executive lobe dysfunction. The most prominent was Gage's obstinate behavior and his limited ability to engage in goal-oriented behavior. According to Harlow's report, Gage "devised many plans of future operations, which are no sooner arranged than they are abandoned."

In the 2004 issue of *Frontiers in Bioscience*, Ken wrote an article about the four most important factors for successfully completing goal-oriented behaviors.

The first, he wrote, is initiation, the starting of actions that move us in a goal-oriented direction. Without this initiation we appear apathetic about life—think of a "couch potato." The second factor is persistence, the ability to stick with an objective until it is successfully completed, even in the presence of distractions. The third involves knowing when the objective has been completed and then stopping in order to not waste resources. (The inability to stop is known as perseveration.) The last factor may be a little tricky to understand. As we are working toward an objective, different circumstances and conditions will arise; some are best ignored. Being able to disregard them and stay on track is essential to achieving a goal, lest we end up "spinning our wheels."

Back in 1951, the neurologist J. M. Nielsen reported that patients with strokes in both the left and right middle (medial) sides of the frontal lobes appeared awake and alert, but unless prompted they neither spoke nor moved.

More recently, Antoine Bechara and colleagues from the Department of Neurology at the University of Iowa's College of Medicine and the Salk Institute of Biological Studies reported, "Following damage to . . . the prefrontal cortex, humans develop a defect in real-life decision making, in spite of otherwise normal intellectual performance. The patients so affected may even realize the consequences of their actions, but fail to act accordingly, thus appearing oblivious to the future" (1996, 215).

What causes some people to dither and seem unmotivated? They move only when something compels them to action. Why do others seem empowered and aggressively pursue long-range goals, even in the absence of immediate needs? It turns out that the brain engages distinct neural networks—different processing modes—for these obviously opposite behaviors. One of them is referred to as the *top-down* or *intentional mode,* and the other, the *bottom-up* or *reactive mode.*

### A Horrific Accident

Lee was raised on a family farm out on the Great Plains. Now the head of that farm and with a family of his own, he is well versed in the rituals and responsibilities of the farmer's way of life. One spring morning, a long-awaited yearly ritual begins: time to plant. Lee clearly faces the known reality that if he wants to harvest a crop at the end of summer and feed his family, he has to get busy plowing and planting. Without being compelled by immediate hunger (in fact, he has quite a hearty breakfast each morning), the tireless Lee goes to work as he has planned. This is the top-down, intentional mode—goal-oriented behavior.

The next winter, something awful happened. Lee was involved in a serious automobile accident and was left badly injured and comatose. Imaging studies revealed that he had large contusions of his frontal lobes. He recovered slowly over the winter months, and by spring, things seemed relatively normal. However, instead of resuming his usual seasonal work routine, he would awaken in the morning and just lie in bed. The interactions between Lee and his wife, Jean, who clearly knew he had to start plowing and planting, would go like this:

"Aren't you going to work today?" Jean would ask.

"Nope," Lee would respond. "I'm just gonna stick around the house."

"Lee, get up, get dressed and start working." When pushed, Lee would get his work clothes on, but then he just sat in front of the television. "Shut it off, get up and go to work," Jean would admonish him. Lee finally did, but without his Jean's continual reminding, he usually stopped before completing all that needed to be done. This is the bottom-up, reactive mode. After the car accident, Lee lost his will or ability for top-down, intentional actions. He could no longer self-initiate goal-oriented actions, but he responded to his wife's demands, a form of bottom-up, reactive behavior.

Normally, most of us maintain a sort of teeter-totter balance between the intentional and reactive behavior modes. Sometimes, though, these systems can be somewhat unbalanced in one direction or the other. As a result, certain individuals are highly motivated by their intentional systems and only mini-mally influenced by what is happening outside them. In other words, like Lee prior to the accident, they have a strong internal drive to accomplish their objectives.

In contrast, other people are not very motivated by their intentional systems and instead are strongly influenced by external stimuli—the things they see, hear, touch, and taste. In Lee's case, his wife was the external stimulus compel-ling him to do what he could no longer initiate on his own.

A person's propensity for acting with intention or, conversely, behaving reactively, is most likely influenced by both genetics and learning. But as we saw with Phineas Gage and Lee, frontal-lobe injury can disrupt the balance between the two systems: reactive behavior dominates, and the individual become stimulus dependent, caught up in reacting to whatever is happening in his immediate environment. At the same time, the person is unable to mus-ter the internal drive to focus on some more meaningful objective outside or beyond the present environment. This is a loss of executive function and is exactly what we could describe about Lee. (This could have been the case with Gage, but those details are less clear.)

Family members of those with frontal-lobe injuries will sometimes complain about annoying stimulus-dependent behaviors, some of which can be demon-strated in the clinic. For example, the French neurologist François Lhermitte described what he called the *environmental dependency syndrome*. Setting down an empty glass and bottle of water in front of patients with frontal lobe dysfunction, without issuing instructions to do anything with them, he noticed they would often fill the glass with water and then drink it. In the same manner, he placed a pad of paper and a pen in front of them, and without asking them to do a thing, he noticed that they would begin writing on the paper.

Ken sees similar behaviors when he examines patients with injured fron-tal lobes (or injury to the frontal lobe connections with the basal ganglia and thalamus). Using different tests, he looks for abnormal adherence or stimulus dependence. For example, he will have patients sit, with eyes closed with their hands on their laps. Then he tells them that when he touches their right hand, they should lift their left hand, and vice versa. He randomly touches either hand and has noticed that people with frontal-lobe injury will typically lift the hand that was touched, rather than the opposite hand as instructed. As you can see, such actions are influenced more by external stimuli than by the will (or ability) to perform the prescribed task correctly.

In another test, Ken asks patients to lift their hand and make a fist. Ken will tell them that when he holds up two fingers they are to raise one finger, and when he holds up one, they are to hold up two. What happens? Those with frontal-lobe disorders routinely exhibit a stimulus-dependent behavior: they raise the same finger or fingers that Ken is holding up, sometimes eventually self-correcting as originally instructed.

Patients with frontal-lobe deficits also can demonstrate a curious condition called echolalia. They automatically repeat what they hear, changing, perhaps, a word or two. For example, if the clinician asks, "How are you feeling?" the patient might respond, "How am I feeling? Well, . . ."

In the delightful children's game "Simon Says," youngsters are supposed to imitate the leader's actions only when he begins an instruction with the words, "Simon says do *this*. . . ." But kids will often mistakenly imitate the examiner's actions after hearing, "Do *this*!" without hearing the "Simon says." Part of the reason this happens is that youngsters still have immature frontal lobes; as a result, their behavior tends to be guided by the actions they see and hear. When they are faced with a choice between a top-down, goal-oriented action and a bottom-up, reactive one, their young minds cannot help but be reactive.

We do not understand entirely how and why the frontal lobes support intentional, goal-oriented actions while inhibiting reactive, stimulus-dependent behaviors. In anatomical and physiologic terms, the frontal lobes are not a homogenous region. Different regions mediate distinct functions. For example, the lateral and dorsomedial portions of the frontal lobes appear to be important in the initiation of long-term goals. However, the extensive (and phenomenal) neuronal connectivity of the frontal lobes may be important in understanding the extent of their functions.

Our cerebral cortex is essentially a six-layered structure containing different kinds of neurons. These neurons form connections with other parts of the cortex (and the areas under it, the subcortical regions). We know that the different cortical areas store distinct forms of knowledge and mediate varying functions, yet they all have the same basic cellular architecture. With this similarity, what allows the cortex to store such diverse forms knowledge and control a range of functions?

The answer is the patterns of connectivity. A sophisticated network of neuronal connections, "modules" if you will, dictates the cognitive processes performed, as well as what information is delivered to, stored in, and distributed from any given area.

Why does this rich connectivity have a bearing on goal-oriented, intentional behaviors and OCD? A quick look at the function and networks of the posterior parietal, temporal, and frontal lobes might be illuminating.

As we mentioned earlier, each of the primary sensory areas in the cerebral cortex receives and analyzes specific information about touch, vision, and hearing from different portions of the thalamus. Recall that each of these cortical areas has connections to parts of the brain called modality specific association cortical areas. These association areas for vision, touch, and hearing contain memories or representations of previously perceived stimuli and also allow us to recognize incoming stimuli. Then all these specific sensory association areas send projections to polymodal areas (Figure 2.5 and Figure 2.6). This polymodal connectivity and integration allows cross-modal associations, such as visual-auditory-touch—associations that enable us to identify those items that we see, hear, or hold. This identification is the basis of symbolic behaviors. For example, when we can hear the word car, we can imagine an automobile and hear the engine roar.

After a frontal-lobe injury like Gage's, the knowledge stored in the sensory association regions does remain intact. When patients with frontal-lobe injury are given tests to assess their knowledge, many will still perform generally as well as an uninjured person.

Studies of those who have had an injury to the frontal-lobes or a severing of the input and output from other parts of the brain to the frontal lobes may reveal no major alteration in knowledge, language, or even general intelligence. As was mentioned, however, they often have a loss of their ability to perform goal-oriented behaviors, with a loss of self-motivation as well as a loss of persistence until the job is finished. People with frontal lobe dysfunction also often have the inability to disengage from performing meaningless behaviors, and this is the primary behavioral deficit underlying adherence disorders.

Remember that after the accident that injured his frontal lobes, Lee plowed the fields and planted crops, but only after his wife's pleadings. Had he not, the family would have eventually gone hungry. When hunger causes blood glucose levels to drop, the hypothalamus (which monitors blood glucose) alerts the cerebral cortex that food is needed. Because of his injury, Lee was not motivated to plant crops. But if his glucose dropped because a lack of food, he would stop the couch-potato behavior and go look for food.

People with frontal-lobe injury continue having biological drives that are activated by bodily needs. Under these conditions they can still initiate actions. Emotions, too, can produce similar actions. The frontal lobes are connected with the amygdala (Figure 6.1), the part of the brain that induces feelings of anger or fear. Normally, our frontal lobes help control the amygdala so that

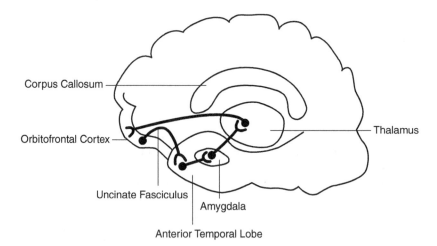

*Figure 6.1* The basolateral limbic circuit. The orbitofrontal cortex connects with the anterior temporal cortex by means of a white-matter pathway called the uncinate fasciculus. The anterior temporal lobe is connected with the amygdala, which is connected with the thalamus. The thalamus sends connections back to the orbitofrontal lobe.

emotions will not overrule our goal-oriented behaviors, but an injury to the frontal lobes can cause a loss of amygdala control. Frustrated or angry individuals with frontal lobe dysfunction might get very aggressive.

Those suffering from frontal dysfunction, as does Lee, know that they must attend to certain needs, such as finding food. They know, too, how to arrange their environments to avoid dangerous situations. But although they can be motivated by immediate biological drives or emotions, they are incapable of *joining* such biological and emotional drives with the stored knowledge for planning and goal achievement. This special synthesis of cognitive knowledge, emotion-based responses, and biological drive states normally is performed via the frontal lobes. This connectivity enables goal-oriented behavior.

## Are We Stuck or Free?

The frontal-lobe behavioral deficits we have been discussing all have something in common. They are all *adherent* behaviors. In other words, the patient's behavior is governed entirely by the present, external stimulus rather than by long-term ambitions. In the clinic, two severe examples of adherence is the *grasp reflex* and *mitgehen*, which can be uncovered during a neurological examination. In the assessment for grasp reflex, the patient will be told to keep his hands relaxed while the clinician runs her finger across his palm. If the reflex is present, the patient will automatically grasp the clinician's finger, despite the instructions to relax the hands. This is not normal for adults. It is often seen, though, in healthy infants, because they do not yet have fully mature, functional frontal lobes. This is an advantage for babies, who can cling more closely to their mothers. But the adult patient becomes a slave, so to speak, to the immediate stimulus (the clinician's finger) and cannot follow the original instructions.

In the assessment for mitgehen, which is German for "going with," the patient is again instructed to keep his or her hands relaxed on the lap. The clinician will then lightly touch one of the patient's fingers with his own. If the clinician then moves his finger, and the patient moves with him to stay in contact, it is a display of mitgehen: The patient *goes with* the examiner's movements and seemingly cannot break free.

In both examples, we can see that the patients are entangled with their immediate environment. Instead of following simple instructions, they automatically respond to a meaningless external stimulus.

Frontal-lobe dysfunction also can involve perseveration. This term comes from the Latin *perseverare,* meaning to persist, remain constant, or persevere in something. Patients with this condition continue to work on or unnecessarily repeat a given task. For example, the Soviet psychologist Alexander Luria asked patients with frontal-lobe damage to do a simple task. He showed them an example of a scribbled "triple loop," gave them pen and paper, and instructed them to draw the same thing. Instead of sketching a triple loop and then stopping, a number of his patients just continued drawing. When asked to pen alternating triangles and squares, other patients repeatedly drew only one of the figures, apparently oblivious to the missing one (Figure 6.2). Once they think they know how to solve a problem, people who perseverate will adhere to that solution, even when it no longer works.[1]

Individuals with OCD often perseverate. Rafael Penadés at the Clinical Institute of Neurosciences in Barcelona along with coworkers studied a group of patients with OCD by administering several tests, including one called the Stroop task. In this test, subjects are shown the names of colors, such as red, green, and blue. However, each word can be printed in either the same or a different color than the name itself indicates. For example, the word *red* might be printed in green. The subject is then asked to state the color he or she sees, but not to read the word itself. Penadés found that participants with OCD, like patients with frontal lobe injuries, tended to err by reading the word instead of stating its color. This is another example of an adherence disorder, an inability to disengage, which again points to frontal-lobe dysfunction.

There is more support for the relationship between a dysfunctional frontal lobe network and OCD. Several studies have demonstrated that people with OCD are impaired on tests that look at the ability to disengage using a specific mental strategy for solving a problem, normally a function of the frontal lobe executive system. This ability to switch strategies when necessary is called cognitive flexibility. One of the most frequently used tests for assessing patients with frontal-lobe dysfunction is the Wisconsin Card Sorting Test. In this test, developed in 1948 by Esta Berg at the University of Wisconsin, the subject is given a deck of cards with geometric figures of varying shapes, colors, and number of objects. The examiner asks the subject to divide the deck into piles of similar cards without saying how to do it. However, the examiner will tell the subject whether the

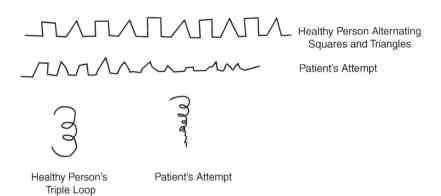

*Figure 6.2* Examples of the types of drawing performance abnormalities observed in patients with frontal-lobe dysfunction. Note that in these examples, the subject starts to perseverate. In the triple loop task, the subject continues to make circles or loops after he or she should have completed the task. In the alternative figure drawing task, after initially alternatively drawing triangles and squares, the patient starts to repeatedly draw the same figure.

strategy by which she is sorting is right or wrong: in other words, the instructions are implied.

Once the subject figures out the right sorting strategy, she continues to use it. But on multiple occasions, the examiner interrupts by declaring that the current sorting strategy is no longer correct. As you might expect, uninjured individuals will try alternative strategies until the examiner tells them that one is correct. Scores are based on the ability to disengage from the current strategy and find an alternative method. People with OCD, however, have difficulty disengaging and changing card-sorting strategies.

## Adherence and Anxiety

While he was at the University of California at Los Angeles, Lewis Baxter and his coworkers (Saxena et al., 1998) used positron emission tomographic function imaging (PET scanning) studies to learn if there is evidence that there was abnormal brain activation in people with OCD. Although functional imaging studies have shown increased activation of the frontal lobes in patients with OCD, specifically the orbitofrontal cortex, what Baxter's finding indicates is not quite clear. In general, investigators conclude that such heightened activity means that the scanned part of the brain plays a major role in processing a given task. However, other studies have shown that as people become more proficient at performing a task, the level of stimulation in a given area deceases. Confusing as it might seem, observing less activity could indicate that the scanned portion of the brain does indeed normally mediate the given function. With all that in mind, investigators have suggested that the increased activation in the orbitofrontal cortex in OCD patients means that rather than growing more proficient, this part of the brain is working extra hard because of its own impairment.

In some studies, patients with OCD are subjected to stress during function imaging studies. For example, the examiner will ask the MRI-sequestered subjects if they remembered to check the door locks at home, or if their hands are clean. Investigators have observed heightened activity in this same orbitofrontal area. Maybe the increased stimulation occurs because the orbitofrontal cortex is not properly modulating the activity of the amygdala, which plays a critical role in our emotional reactions, such as fear and anxiety, and these people's brains are attempting to compensate. When patients with OCD are successfully treated, they demonstrate a decrease of activation in in this region.

In MRI studies of OCD patients, investigators who measured the size of brain structures found reduced amounts of gray matter in the frontal lobes (and thus fewer neurons), which could help explain why people with OCD have problems disengaging from thoughts and obsessions.[2]

As a physician, Ken is pretty obsessive and compulsive about certain things. Throughout any given day he might find himself concerned about his patients, whether he failed to ask them important assessment-related questions, if he forgot to perform some part of his examination or order an important test, if he should have considered other diagnoses, or if he had determined the optimal treatment. He always checks his patients' laboratory work carefully and can become upset if something is amiss. Similarly, he rechecks his notes to assure himself they are complete and can get agitated if he inadvertently forgets to convey important information in a communication with colleagues. Sound obsessive?

In other areas of his life, Ken has few if any such obsessions or compulsions. In clinic, he cleans his hands all day long, before seeing each patient, but otherwise he typically just washes them before eating and after visiting the men's room. Moreover, he does not routinely check door locks or stove burners, or look under his bed before going to sleep. It would appear, then, that his obsessive compulsive disorder is specific to his work domain and is based on rational reasoning. He has never been treated for OCD, nor does he plan to be because his medical-related obsessions and compulsions are simply the characteristics of a good physician—not symptoms of a dysfunctional frontal executive system. In fact, they are probably evidence of a well-functioning executive system that is spontaneously planning and problem solving.

In a similar way, many of us who are very religious may not suffer from OCD, but we could have domain-specific obsessions and compulsions. And like Ken's work habits, certain obsessive compulsive religious behaviors may very well have a positive influence on family and friends.

Although there are similarities between OCD and being very religious, there are also important differences. As mentioned, people with OCD are always trying to stop obsessing and behaving compulsively; because of this, they live in almost constant struggle. In contrast, the very religious will sometimes talk about the great joy they derive from their beliefs and their acts of worship. Unlike those with OCD who can agonize over their obsessions, some of the faithful do become anxious and frustrated when they cannot adhere to the rituals and routines they know and so scrupulously follow.

## Getting Hooked

Music, chants, and repeated prayers are an important part of worship and can offer what some believe is an unsurpassed peace. For reasons not entirely understood, these activities sometimes engender an emotional high, even euphoria.

As we mentioned earlier, Olds and Milner inserted electrodes into the brains of rats and discovered that when the rodents simply pressed a lever that stimulated the region around the nucleus accumbens, they were somehow compelled to keep pressing it—even without any external reward and for no apparent reason. So compelling was this drive that even hungry rats ignored the levers for food and water in order to continue pushing this particular lever. We now know the brain region being activated, the nucleus accumbens, is a part of the reward network.

Recall that the frontal lobes are critical to mediating executive functions and goal-oriented behaviors. In Chapter 4 we also reviewed the reward center (the nucleus accumbens–ventral striatal network) and mentioned that this reward network does receive input from portions of the frontal lobes. This reward network also projects back to the frontal lobes. Because the frontal lobes are responsible for formulating long-term goals and activating the motor system to pursue these goals, the ventral striatal reward network together with the frontal lobe executive network could act as a kind of feedback loop. Thus an accomplishment would activate this reward system and provide critical, positive, "goal-accomplished" input back to the frontal executive system. It is no surprise that this system is also activated by commonly abused substances, such as cocaine and amphetamines. These drugs are analogous to the stimulation given by Olds and Milner. Substance abuse prompts obsessive compulsive behavior. Is addiction somehow similar to certain incessant actions of highly religious people who feel compelled to forgo many of life's pleasures for some form of heavenly reward?

Menon and Levitin (2005) at the Department of Psychiatry and Behavioral Sciences at Stanford University School of Medicine performed a study in which subjects listened to music. The researchers found a related increased activity in the reward-processing network, including the midbrain, which manufactures and directs dopamine to the nucleus accumbens. In addition, they also discovered changes in the insula (Figure 6.3). The insula is a region of the cerebral cortex that helps to control the autonomic nervous system and thus influences heart rate and blood pressure. The activity of the autonomic nervous system plays an important role in emotional experiences.

Some evidence that religiosity and addiction might both activate this neural reward network is illustrated by the story of William Griffith Wilson, better known as Bill W., whose promising career on Wall Street was ruined by alcohol. Day after day, he remained almost constantly drunk and, as a result, mostly incapacitated. In 1934, a friend with the same problem introduced Bill to an alleged "spiritual cure" for alcoholism, an evangelical Christian movement referred to as the Oxford Group. The group did not consider itself a religion and had neither clergy nor churches, but its members strived to adhere to what they believed to be God's plan. They viewed themselves as modern crusaders whose goal was to develop a "A new world order for Christ the King."

During his immersion in this movement, Bill was administered a hallucinogenic concoction known as the belladonna cure, at the Charles B. Towns Hospital, a detoxification facility for alcoholics. He claimed to have had a spiritual experience and subsequently quit drinking.

Bill became convinced that the power to overcome his alcohol addiction came purely through the invited grace of a higher spiritual power. After about a year in the Oxford Group, Bill met Robert Holbrook Smith, also known as Dr. Bob, a medical doctor and fellow member of the movement, who similarly was able to halt his alcohol abuse by becoming highly spiritual. With this connection, they cofounded Alcoholics Anonymous, better known as AA. Now convinced that alcoholism is an illness caused by an overwhelming obsession with consuming alcohol, Bill and Dr. Bob were quick to incorporate into AA the idea of alcoholism as an obsessive-compulsive illness.

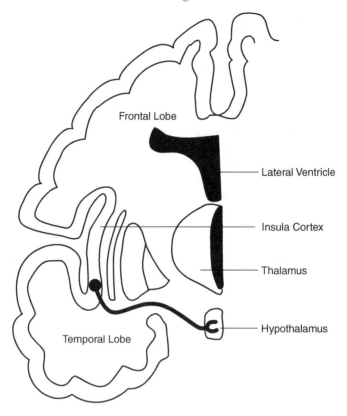

*Figure 6.3*  The insula. This diagram of a coronal section (side to side) through the brain reveals the insular cortex, the hypothalamus, and their connections. The hypothalamus helps control the autonomic nervous and endocrine, or hormonal, systems through its connections with the pituitary gland. This hypothalamic pituitary network helps to control blood pressure and heart rate.

AA has continued to use one of the most successful methods for treating alcoholism. Critical to the participants' success in abating their alcoholic compulsion is absolute adherence to the Twelve-Step Program, a practice that involves an admission of addiction and of being powerless without God's help. Regular attendance is a must. Adherents must routinely declare: *We*

1. *Admitted we were powerless over alcohol—that our lives had become unmanageable.*
2. *Came to believe that a Power greater than ourselves could restore us to sanity.*
3. *Made a decision to turn our will and our lives over to the care of God as we understood Him.*
4. *Made a searching and fearless moral inventory of ourselves.*

5. *Admitted to God, to ourselves and to other human beings the exact nature of our wrongs.*
6. *Were entirely ready to have God remove all these defects of character.*
7. *Humbly asked Him to remove our shortcomings.*
8. *Made a list of all persons we had harmed, and became willing to make amends to them all.*
9. *Made direct amends to such people wherever possible, except when to do so would injure them or others.*
10. *Continued to take personal inventory and when we were wrong promptly admitted it.*
11. *Sought through prayer and meditation to improve our conscious contact with God, as we understood Him, praying only for knowledge of His will for us and the power to carry that out.*
12. *Having had a spiritual awakening as the result of these steps, we will try to carry this message to alcoholics, and to practice these principles in all our affairs.*

Another organization, Narcotics Anonymous, maintains a nonreligious stance. This group claims not to be a religious organization or fellowship, but at meetings members admit their addiction and tell their stories, confessing their addiction-caused transgressions, not unlike confessing sins.

Do such meetings with quasi-religious rituals, confessions, and new obsessive behaviors allow people to end substance abuse because they are replacing a harmful form of addiction with one that is safe? Is scrupulosity, that disorder of constant fearful obsession and guilt over moral or religious issues, another means of stimulating the nucleus accumbens–reward network? We do not know for certain, but the idea is worthy of our consideration.

## Notes

1. There is even more support for the relationship between a dysfunctional frontal-lobe network and OCD. Frontal mediated disengagement allows normal people to switch strategies when necessary called cognitive flexibility. For further evidence of the cognitive inflexibility associated with OCD, see S. Bannon et al., "Processing Impairments in OCD: It Is More than Inhibition!" *Behaviour Research and Therapy* 46, no. 6 (June 2008): 689–700; S. R. Chamberlain et al., "The Neuropsychology of Obsessive Compulsive Disorder: The Importance of Failures in Cognitive and Behavioural Inhibition as Candidate Endophenotypic Markers," *Neuroscience & Biobehavioral Reviews* 29, no. 3 (May 2005): 399–419.
2. There is an additional explanation of this increased activity in the ventral-orbital-frontal cortex and its association with OCD. Besides the connections with the temporal and parietal regions, the motor cortex, and portions of the limbic system, the frontal lobes have strong connections to the basal ganglia. These connections are specific for certain areas of the frontal lobe. For example, Alexander and his coworkers (1986) described several non-motor basal ganglia circuits. These non-motor circuits include output from the basal ganglia to two frontal cortical areas: the dorsal lateral prefrontal cortex and the orbital-ventral prefrontal cortex. These prefrontal-basal ganglia circuits appear to be modular or independent. In one of these

networks, the orbital-ventral prefrontal cortex projects to the ventral caudate. In the other network, the dorsolateral cortex projects to the dorsal caudate.

In animal studies, Iversen and Mishkin (1970) found that when they ablated monkeys' lateral (convexity) frontal lobes, the monkeys became perseverative. Divac et al. (1967) found that experimental animals also became perseverative when the ventral caudate was ablated. These perseverative behavioral deficits are very similar to those observed in humans with OCD. Thus the preservative deficit for which the orbitofrontal lobes are attempting to compensate by increasing their activity may also be related to deficits in the basal ganglia–thalamic networks. This deficit or dysfunction may be structural or related to abnormalities of the neurotransmitter systems that modulate these networks.

# 7  Circle the Wagons
## Depression, Fear, and Aggression

*For everything there is a season, and a time for every matter under heaven: a time to be born, and a time to die; a time to plant, and a time to pluck up what is planted; a time to kill, and a time to heal; a time to break down, and a time to build up; a time to weep, and a time to laugh; a time to mourn, and a time to dance.*

—Ecclesiastes 3:1–4

## Quality of Life

All animals, including humans, strive to improve their quality of life. Many factors can influence a person's quality of life, including being able to fulfill biological needs such as food and water, avoiding pain, and finding comfort. However, one of the most important factors in the quality of a person's life are moods and emotions. Thus, humans are strongly motivated to avoid sadness and depression as well as to seek joy, happiness, and euphoria. Religious and spiritual activities and beliefs can strongly influence mood and emotions. In this chapter we discuss some of the relationships between emotions and religious beliefs.

Some surveys suggest that at least 20 percent of the American population will suffer from serious depression sometime during life. Some of the major symptoms of depressive disorder include feelings of sadness, gloom, and melancholy; an inability to enjoy life (anhedonia); not looking forward to future events; a change in eating habits, such as loss of appetite or an increased appetite with a cravings for carbohydrates; a change in sleeping habits, such as increased sleep or early morning awakenings (say, 4:30 A.M.); and a reduction of sexual interest.

It is normal to develop symptoms of depression when a family member dies, or we are separated from a loved one, or where we fail to achieve an important goal, or if we are told that we have a serious or terminal illness. Many people would call this normal grieving rather than depression, but grief that is disabling and prolonged is clearly depression.

Lawson Reed Wulsin and his coworkers at the University of Cincinnati and Harold G. Koenig at Duke University have performed studies revealing that religious involvement reduces depressive symptoms. Lloyd Balbuena and his coworkers at the University of Saskatchewan studied the influence of religious attendance and spirituality on depression in more than 12,000 Canadians over a period of 14 years. Balbuena and his associates found that whereas religious attendance was associated with a reduction of depression, spirituality had no influence on depression. The reasons that religious involvement can decrease the severity of depression are not entirely known. However, to understand how religiosity influences depression it might help to try to understand some the brain mechanisms that may cause the signs and symptoms of depression. Unfortunately, these mechanisms are not fully understood, but we will discuss several major theories.

### Psychoanalytic Theory

One of the first modern theories about depression was provided by Sigmund Freud, who wrote that depression is a response to a loss, such as the loss of a loved one or a failure to achieve a goal. According to this psychoanalytic theory, such a loss or failure triggers unconscious self-anger, which weakens the person's ego. Weakening of the ego results in self-hate, which becomes manifest as depression. Self-hate may explain why people who are severely depressed may commit suicide.

Kanita Dervic and her coworkers at Columbia University in New York studied suicide rates in people who were religious versus those who were not. They found that religious people had a lower rate of suicide. However, the reason that being religious reduces the rate of suicide is not fully known. Some religions teach that suicide is a sin; as bad as someone's suffering and pain from depression may be, hell would be worse. Religions also teach forgiveness and God's love for his creation. These beliefs may help reduce self-anger and self-hate. However, as we will see, there are other possible reasons that religious practices may reduce the prevalence of depression, the severity of depression, and the rate of suicide.

### Neurotransmitter Theory

In the brain, nerves communicate with each other by giving off chemicals that can either excite neighboring neurons or inhibit the excitement of neighboring neurons. These chemicals are called neurotransmitters because they transfer information from one nerve cell to another. In the past 50 years we have learned that certain medications that increase the levels of serotonin and/or norepinephrine can alleviate depression; however, the means by which changes in these neurotransmitter levels improve mood is still not entirely known.

Meditation has much in common with certain forms of prayer. Hideho Arita at the Toho University School of Medicine studied people who were practicing Zen meditation and found that meditation reduced negative moods. The nerve cells that produce serotonin and norepinephrine are located in the brain stem, but the frontal cortex can modulate the activity of these neurons. Arita found that during meditation, frontal activation took place and was associated with an increase in serotonin.

### The Reward System: The Ventral Striatum

Earlier we discussed the ventral striatum, the reward network that includes the nucleus accumbens, and the olfactory tubercle, as well as the ventral portions of the caudate nucleus and putamen. Jane Epstein and her co-investigators at Cornell University performed functional imaging in people with depression. They found that unlike the non-depressed subjects, when patients with depression are presented positive (rewarding) stimuli, they demonstrate a decrease in activation of their reward system (nucleus accumbens–ventral striatum system). This decreased activation of the reward system correlates with these participants' decreased interest in performing activities and the decreased rewarding pleasure they experience when performing some activities.

Uffe Schjødt and coworkers used functional magnetic resonance imaging (fMRI) to investigate how the brain is altered when a group of Danish Christians (the Protestant Danish Christian Church) engaged in prayer. The researchers found that these subjects' prayers did activate the striatal reward system. This is another reason that religious practices such as prayer may help alleviate depression.

### Lesion Studies

One of the oldest and still one of the best means of learning how the brain works is to study patients who have an injury to a portion of the brain to learn how this type of injury influences these patients' behavior. For example, in 1861, Paul Broca reported that left hemisphere lesions are most likely to impair patients' ability to produce speech most often had stroke damage to the left hemisphere. From this observation, he concluded that in right-handed people, the left hemisphere is dominant for mediating—programming—speech and language. In 1939, in his classic book, *The Organism: A Holistic Approach to Biology*, Kurt Goldstein reported that patients who had left-hemisphere strokes that damaged the frontal lobe often had severe depression. He called this the "catastrophic reaction." The famous neurologist Joseph Babinski was probably the first to report, in 1914, that patients with right-hemisphere injury often appeared indifferent or euphoric. Other investigators have confirmed Babinski's observations. In contrast to left-hemispheric lesions, patients with right-frontal-hemispheric strokes often demonstrated apathy and indifference. In one of the most extensive studies, Guido Gainotti in Rome studied patients with right- and left-hemisphere strokes and supported this left-hemisphere injury-depression versus right-hemisphere injury-indifference-or-euphoria hemispheric dichotomy. The depressive reaction associated with left-hemisphere disease usually is seen in patients with injury to the lower lateral portion of their frontal lobes.

Because people develop negative moods when the left hemisphere is not functioning normally, the left hemisphere must be important in mediating positive moods. In addition, since many people will experience positive moods and emotions when the right hemisphere is damaged, the right hemisphere appears to be important in mediating negative emotions and moods. This hemispheric mood dichotomy has been supported by Richard Davidson of the University of Wisconsin, who studied uninjured healthy people. Davidson used an electroencephalogram (EEG) to learn whether alterations in the brain activity of the frontal lobes occur when these healthy people experience positive versus negative emotions. Davidson found that with positive emotions there was left-hemispheric activation, and with negative emotions right-hemisphere activation. These results were consistent with the emotional changes associated with stroke, such that positive emotions are associated with greater left- than right-frontal-hemisphere activation and negative emotions with greater right- than left-frontal-hemispheric activation. Using functional imaging, G. P. Lee and co-investigators from the Medical College of Georgia found similar results. They observed activation of the left dorsolateral frontal regions during the experience of positive emotions, and activation of the right dorsolateral frontal regions during the experience of negative emotions. Using functional imaging of the brain, C. J. Bench and coworkers from the Royal Free Hospital and School of Medicine in London studied patients who were depressed and found a reduction of activity in the anterior lateral frontal lobes, especially in the left hemisphere.

We mentioned that patients who are suffering from depression have a serotonin deficiency. It is possible that depression might be more common with left-hemisphere than right-hemisphere strokes because there may be asymmetrical control of neurotransmitter systems, the left hemisphere being dominant in activating the serotonergic neurotransmitter system. This asymmetry hypothesis was supported by Helen Mayberg, who reported in 1988 that after a left-hemisphere stroke with depression, there is a reduction of serotonergic receptor binding.

Although alterations of neurotransmitters, left-hemispheric dysfunction, and deactivation of the ventral striatal accumbens reward network all appear to play an important role in the pathophysiology of depression, these observations do not explain fully why religious activity can reduce depression.

Psychotherapy works as well as antidepressant medications for treating people with depression. During psychotherapy, the depressed patient is encouraged to speak while the therapist listens. Many people with depression isolate themselves and have fewer social interactions. Speech activates the left frontal lobe; perhaps this activation helps to reduce depression. Going to a house of worship frequently encourages social interaction and speech. Perhaps these social interactions also may help people who are suffering from depression. In addition, when life is a living hell, the promise of heaven is a gift.

## Depression, Religion, and Health

Much has been written about the positive effects of religion, prayer, and meditation on health. Harold Koenig and his coworkers at Duke (1999b) studied almost 4,000 older adults in the Piedmont area of North Carolina. Over a 6.3-year period, the researchers found that of those who regularly attended church, 22.9 percent died, but of those who did not attend church regularly, 37.4 percent died. Thus, the people who were religious and attended church were less likely to die. As mentioned above, Harold Koenig (1999a) also demonstrated that attending church reduced depression.

Studies have revealed that the presence of depression can reduce cancer survival. It has been reported that religiosity and/or spirituality improved the survival rate of women with breast cancer. For example, Peter H. van Ness and his colleagues reported that women who attended church once a week had a 32 percent reduction in the risk of mortality compared with those who never attended religious services. The same appears to holds true of heart failure. For example, psychological depression appears to contribute to worse medical outcomes in patients with heart failure. This finding ranks depression with such risk factors as high cholesterol, hypertension, and even the ability of the heart to pump blood throughout the body. J. A. Blumenthal and coworkers from Duke and the University of North Carolina found that depressed patients were over 50 percent more likely to die or be hospitalized for their heart disease than patients who had similar conditions but were not depressed.

Investigators have postulated several reasons that patients with these medical conditions who have depression do worse than those without depression. Depression is often associated with anxiety and stress. With stress and anxiety, the body secretes hormones that increase the work of the heart and increase the activity of the sympathetic nervous system. The sympathetic nervous system normally activates when we are in danger and prepares the body of fight or flight. These changes include an increase blood pressure and heart rate, factors that also put stress on the heart.

With depression and stress, the body secretes increased levels of cortisol into the bloodstream. Suzanne C. Segerstrom and Gregory E. Miller from the University of Kentucky reviewed more than 300 articles over a 30-year period that studied the relationship between stress and the human immune system and concluded that chronic stress with elevated levels of cortisol can reduce immune responses. Increased cortisol levels can also be toxic to some tissues. For example, as reviewed by Lupien and coworkers from McGill University, increased cortisol levels injure the nerve cells in the hippocampus, a region that is critical for the formation of new memories. This area often degenerates in patients who have Alzheimer's disease. Yakir Kaufman with coworkers from Toronto found that people with high levels of religious practices experienced a slower progression of this disease.

## The Wolves Are Outside: Fear and Aggression

According to the United Nations 1948 Genocide Convention and the 1987 Genocide Convention Implementation Act, the definition of genocide is an "act committed with intent to destroy, in whole or in part, a national, ethnic, racial or religious group, including, killing its members; causing them serious bodily or mental harm; deliberately inflicting on a group conditions of life calculated to bring about their physical destruction in whole or in part; imposing measures intended to prevent births within the group; and forcibly transferring children of the group to another group."

When people hear the term *genocide*, they often think about the Nazi Holocaust, during which Christians in Germany, Austria, Poland, and several other European countries killed 6 million people because they were Jews, Gypsies, homosexuals, or others who were considered undesirable. Genocide, however, occurred before and after the Holocaust.

Although factors such as money, food, land, and power may lead to war, the common denominator of many genocidal acts is religious intolerance, based on differences in religious beliefs, practices, and cultures. For example, Jews were persecuted, tortured, and killed during the Inquisition in Spain during the fourteenth century and this genocide lasted to the eighteenth century. Recent genocides have targeted other groups. More than a million Armenian Christians were massacred by the Muslim Turks during 1915–16. During the 1990s, hundreds of thousands of Muslims in Bosnia-Herzegovina were killed, primarily by Serbian Orthodox Christians.

Even the Old Testament has several stories of genocide. For example, after exiting Egypt, the Hebrews, led by Moses, encountered the Midianites, who worshiped idols. As written in Numbers 31:7–18, the Lord commanded Moses to kill every Midianite man. And so it was done. The Hebrews captured the Midianite women and children and took all the Midianites' animal herds, flocks, and material goods as plunder. They then burned all the Midianite towns.

The fate of the ancient Canaanites was even worse. The promised land of Israel was already inhabited by a group of people who were not Hebrews. The book of Deuteronomy (7:1–2) states, "When the Lord your God brings you into the land you are entering to possess and drives out before you many nations . . . then you must destroy them totally. Make no treaty with them and show them no mercy." A later verse reads, "[D]o not leave alive anything that breathes. Completely destroy them . . . as the Lord your God has commanded you" (Deuteronomy 20:16).

Even within the same religion, different sects practice forms of genocide. For example, both Catholics and Protestants are Christians, but there have been genocides within Christianity. Although many people attribute the Great Irish Famine (1845–52), which killed more than 1 million Irish Catholics, to the potato blight, the Catholic Irish were terribly abused by Protestant Britain. By law, the Irish Catholics were prohibited from owning their own land. They could not vote or hold any political office. They were not allowed to be educated and could not enter any profession. Even the major university in Ireland, Trinity College, had restrictions on Irish Catholics that prevented them from being members of the college until late in the nineteenth century. Before and during the famine, Ireland's Catholics lived in poverty; for the most part, they were the tenant farmers for absentee Protestant landlords. Although some of these laws were changed just before the famine, the primary food of the Irish Catholics was the potato; when the crop failed, they starved. Whereas the Irish Catholics were not killed outright by the Protestant British, British actions and policy contributed to the famine. According to one story, even the Muslim leader of the Ottoman empire, Sultan Abdülmecid, tried to send the starving Irish Catholics large sums of money so they could buy food, but Queen Victoria objected. Overall, the Great Irish Famine could very well constitute a genocide as legally defined by the United Nations.

Today, in Middle Eastern countries such as Iraq, Muslims are killing other Muslims. The people who are being killed by bombs and gun are not soldiers but civilians, including women and children. Why would these two groups of people want to kill one another? Both groups believe in Allah and the teachings of the Prophet Muhammad. Both strictly adhere to the laws written in the same holy book, the Quran. The Prophet had no sons but did have a daughter, Fatima. Fatima married the Prophet's cousin Ali. Because Ali was the Prophet's closest male relative, many Muslims thought and still think that after Muhammad's death Ali should be their leader. However, Muhammad also had a close friend named Abu Bakr. Other Muslims believed and continue to believe that Abu Bakr was their true leader. The followers of Abu Bakr are called Sunni Muslims; those who follow Ali are called Shiite Muslims. Although Ali was killed by followers of Abu Bakr about 1,300 years ago, many Sunni Muslims want to rid the world of Shiites—and vice versa. And so the killing goes on.

Earlier, we mentioned that most people who are brought up in a certain religion remain loyal to that religion. We attributed this loyalty in part to the phenomenon called imprinting. However, there are other reasons for peoples' loyalty to a religion and abhorrence of people who practice other religions.

Most often people remain loyal to their religion for positive reasons. Their religious beliefs and practices bring them joy, relief from suffering, friendship, and many other benefits in this life. They believe that in return for their faith, they will win future rewards, such as heaven. The vast majority of clerics teach charity, peoplehood, and love. Many clerics bring people into their flock by positive means, being teachers, advisors, comforters, therapists, and friends. However, besides positive reasons for religious loyalty, there are also negative reasons. History is full of incidents of religious intolerance and hatred of those who act and believe differently. This hatred is often accompanied by aggressive behavior. Some clerics even keep people in their flock by convincing them that there are "wolves outside."

The brain mechanisms that mediate the emotion of anger and associated aggressive behaviors are still not entirely known. Researchers have learned much by studying patients with neurological diseases. When Ken was training to be a neurologist at the Harvard Neurological Unit of Boston City Hospital, Dr. Vernon Mark was the Chief of Neurosurgery. At this time, Ken was the Chief Resident of the Harvard Neurological Service at Boston City Hospital, a medical student named Michael Crichton (who later became a famous author) rotated on to the Neurology Service. Ken brought Michael to a Neurosurgical

Department conference at Boston City Hospital, at which Dr. Mark was presenting a patient. This young woman was being evaluated for a form of epilepsy. Among the first signs of an oncoming seizure were outbursts of rage and the performance of violent acts. During these episodes of rage, the woman would throw objects and pound items with her fists, often hurting herself and sometimes others. These outbursts were not provoked by other people but occurred spontaneously. When she was not having these rage episodes, the patient was very pleasant and agreeable.

Dr. Mark placed electrodes in the patient's amygdala (Figures 4.5 and 6.1) and recorded from these electrodes. He found that during these attacks of rage, the amygdala would fire abnormally, a focal seizure. After Dr. Mark became certain that these discharges were the cause of the patient's rage attacks, with her permission he surgically removed this area of her brain, and her violent rages abated.

It was apparent that Michael Crichton was fascinated by this patient. Ken told him that although this was an interesting case, rage and aggression from a seizure were very uncommon. Michael seemed so intrigued that Ken asked whether he intended to become a neurologist. Michael told Ken that he did not plan to practice medicine. Rather, he was using his experiences in medical school as material for the books and screenplays he was going to write. About three years after graduating from Harvard Medical School, Michael Crichton wrote a novel called *The Terminal Man*, which also was made into a movie. The protagonist is Harry Benson, an epileptic who beats people up during the beginning of his seizures. The story is very similar to what Michael saw and heard at this conference.

We have other evidence that the amygdala is critical for inducing the emotions of fear and anger. For example, Fredrik Ahs and his coworkers took functional images of healthy subjects' brains while they were viewing spiders or snakes, creatures that people often fear and want to kill. The study revealed that the amygdala does increase its activity in these situations.

Fear, anger, and aggressive behaviors are not always taught. For example, one of Ken's colleagues and co-investigators, Bob Watson, was performing behavioral research with Old World monkeys (macaques). The macaques were born in the laboratory and had never seen a snake. In addition, since birth, these monkeys lived in the same area as their mothers. Their mothers had never been exposed to snakes, either. Being monkeys, their mothers could not verbally tell their children, "Watch out for snakes. Snakes can bite and poison you." Bob wanted to test how well these monkeys could see and attend to visual stimuli presented on their right and left sides. He did not want to use food, because food can often be detected by smell. Bob brought a toy snake into the laboratory and showed it to the monkeys, while he moved the snake to imitate slithering, the monkeys reacted with a combination of panic and aggression. That these monkeys, who had never seen a snake, demonstrated this panic-aggressive response suggests that fear of snakes probably is genetically programmed.

S.M., the 44-year-old mother of three children, is neither a snake handler nor an adventurer, but when handling snakes, she experiences no fear. The fearless S.M. has a rare genetic disease that causes degeneration of the amygdala nuclei in both the right and left temporal lobes. S.M. told investigators at the University of Iowa that about 15 years before, while walking through a park, a man jumped up from a park bench, pressed a knife to her throat, and hissed, "I'm going to cut you." She heard a church choir practicing nearby and calmly told him, "If you're going to kill me, you're going to have to go through my God's angels first." When the man let her go, she walked rather than ran home. In an article about S.M., Justin Feinstein and his coauthors from the University of Iowa (2010) suggested that her lack of fear when the knife was being held to her throat may have panicked her attacker.

With the evidence of these and many other observations and reports, investigators and clinicians have concluded that besides being important for inducing the emotions of fear and anger, the amygdala nucleus helps to prepare and enable the human or animal to fight or flee, actions that are often critical for survival. But what does the amygdala have to do with religious intolerance, hatred of people with different religious beliefs, and genocide?

Religious groups are different not only because they have different theologies but also because they have different cultures. Merely standing in an airport and observing how different people dress may allow a person to learn these people's religion. For example, we might see a woman wearing a hijab, which covers the head and chest. Even if she is not boarding a plane to the Middle East, we would know immediately that most likely she is a Muslim. A man wearing a skull cap, or yarmulke, probably is an Orthodox Jew. A man wearing a cotton turban and a beard is likely to be a Sikh. However, dress is only one of the cultural differences that define different religious cultures. Other factors are what is and is not permissible to eat and drink. For example, eating pork is forbidden to Muslim and Jews. Both Muslims and some fundamentalist Protestants are forbidden to drink alcohol.

The list of religious cultural differences is almost endless, from birth control to polygamy, from circumcision to the type of coffin in which a body is buried—or even whether the body is buried or cremated. Some religions do not allow blood transfusions, even in cases where a person's life is in danger. Because of all these differences, when some of us see someone who is very different, we may perceive their behavior as aberrant. Aberrant behaviors often elicit disdain, annoyance, disgust, or even anger, prompting activation of the fight or flight alarm via the amygdala.

In a study using functional imaging (fMRI), Carl Schwartz from Massachusetts General Hospital and his co-investigators showed healthy subjects pictures of people known to the participants versus pictures of people they did not know. The researchers found that the novel faces activated the amygdala. Elizabeth A. Phelps and her co-investigators at MIT studied Caucasian participants' brains with functional imaging while showing the participants pictures of the faces of Caucasians and African Americans. These investigators found that the Caucasian participants had greater amygdala activation when seeing African Americans whom they did not know than when viewing other Caucasians whom they did not know.

Throughout history, genocide has not been limited to killing people of different religions but can also be based on race or even on subrace. People of different religions also are often members of different races or subraces. For example, Caucasians have been divided into Nordic, Alpine, and Mediterranean peoples. The members of each of these subraces may have different physical features as well as different religions. For example, in Hitler's Germany, Jews, who were primarily Mediterranean-Semitic, were often physically different from the "Aryan Germans," who were often Nordic, with many Jews having darker eyes, darker hair, and darker skin than the Nordic "Aryans."

As we have discussed above, unfamiliarity, either religious or racial, activates the amygdala, the organ of fear and anger. This response to novelty is normal, because when a human or animal sees or hears something unfamiliar, they cannot know at first glance whether that new person or animal is or is not a predator or foe.

Every holy book has a commandment similar to "Thou shall not kill." Every holy book abhors violence against others. But the violent acts visited on innocent populations over the past several thousand years has almost always been committed by highly religious people, if not outright fanatics. For example, the men responsible for the attacks on the United States of September 11, 2001, were all reported to be highly religious Muslims. Some people reflexively (and incorrectly) associate Islam with violence, but as we have discussed, highly religious people of other faiths also have performed terribly violent acts and even genocide against those who believed differently.

When we attempted to find systematic studies of the relationship between violence and religiosity, we could not find many studies where investigators compared highly religious peoples' fear or anger responses to unfamiliar stimuli with the responses of people who were less religious or not religious. We did, however find a study by Christopher Schreck, who along with his coworkers from Rochester Institute of Technology found that peoples' religiosity was correlated with violent victimization.

Anita Fernander from the College of Medicine at the University of Kentucky and her co-investigators studied religiosity in a prison population. They found that prisoners who had committed acts of violence were more religious than those who were imprisoned for other crimes. In addition, Rebecca Socolar, a pediatrician at the University of North Carolina, and her coworkers studied the prevalence of parents who spank and hit their children that belong to different Christian denominations. These investigators reported that conservative and fundamentalist Protestants, and especially those who believe in biblical literalism or inerrancy, spank, hit, and/or physically abuse their children more commonly than those parents who belonged to the more liberal Christian denominations. Thus, violence cannot be entirely explained by an amygdala that is activated in response to unfamiliarity. Perhaps highly religious people who believe in biblical literalism and inerrancy have a greater propensity for aggressive behaviors than do less religious people. If so, why?

Recall that the amygdala is a part of a circuit called the Yakolov or basolateral limbic circuit (Figure 6.1). Also recall that this circuit includes the orbitofrontal cortex, which is connected to the amygdala by a white-matter pathway, called the uncinate fasciculus, and the anterior temporal lobe. Juha Tiihonen, together with coworkers, studied a group of violent offenders by measuring the gray matter of different areas of their cerebral cortex. The researchers found that two of the most common areas to have a less gray matter in these violent people were the frontal lobes, including the orbitofrontal cortex. Experimental studies in monkeys have confirmed that the orbitofrontal cortex is important in the control of anger and aggressiveness. For example, Alicia Izquierdo and coworkers from California State University in Los Angeles found that monkeys with an orbitofrontal lesion had increased aggressiveness when they saw humans, whereas monkeys whose amygdalas had been destroyed had a reduction in their aggressive responses.

In an earlier chapter, we noted that the similarities between several of the behaviors exhibited by people with OCD and those exhibited by religious fundamentalists. We also mentioned that people with OCD might also have defects in their orbitofrontal lobes. Thus, it remains possible that some people with strong fundamentalist religious beliefs and practices have anomalies of the orbitofrontal cortex and that these orbitofrontal anomalies increase strict obsessive compulsive religiosity as well as a proclivity for aggressiveness, especially toward people who are perceived as different. The strongest evidence against this postulate is, however, the observations that many religious fundamentalists are gentle, loving, and tolerant, with no history of aggressiveness. Unfortunately, currently there are no studies of the orbitofrontal cortex in those who engage and support genocide or those who, in contrast, have engaged in great humanitarian efforts. This issue remains unresolved.

# 8    The Genius Beyond Religious Fundamentalism

*Learn from yesterday, live for today, hope for tomorrow. The important thing is not to stop questioning.*
> —Albert Einstein*; Relativity: The Special and the General Theory*

## Questioning, Wondering, Doubting

Ken's mother, Rosalind Golin, was born about the time of the Wright brothers' first successful venture into the skies. Before she died in 1992, she had flown in commercial jetliners to almost every place on this planet. By her middle age, television was a technological breakthrough: not only could Rosalind view news from around the world, she also watched Neil Armstrong and Buzz Aldrin walk on the moon. In 1938, when Ken was but months old, he developed bacterial meningitis. It was serendipity that his pediatrician, a faculty member at the College of Physicians and Surgeons, was testing a new, hopeful treatment for bacterial infections. Because he was quite concerned about baby Ken's condition, the doctor elected to treat him with this experimental medicine; fortunately, Ken regained his full health. Known as sulfanilamides or sulfa drugs, several forms of this medicine continue to be used, even now. A short time later, the widely effective antibiotic penicillin was introduced. And today, of course, even more effective treatments are available for infections like Ken's.

Creativity, it seems, has always played an important role for humans. Tens of thousands of years ago, certain early humans refused to give up their stone spearheads. Others, observing stone's shortcomings, searched for new solutions and experimented with bone and antler (which were more easily shaped and lighter in weight). Rock walls sprang to life with paintings, and jewelry adornments were carefully fashioned from ordinary objects previously ignored. Simple weapons were supplanted by more complex instruments with multiple parts and greater capability; the notions of planting instead of gathering, and breeding captive animals rather than hunting them, took hold.

Ages later, Copernicus, doubting the prevalent explanations of an earth-centered universe, developed the theory of planetary motion around a central sun—the solar system. Subsequently confirmed by Galileo, this was a dramatic advancement of knowledge. During the past several hundred years, many other dramatic, creative advances have taken place, including Newton's classical mechanics, Darwin's theory of evolution, Mendel's genetic theory, Pasteur's germ theory, and Einstein's theory of relativity.

We have altered our environments and enhanced our well-being unlike any other life form on earth. This unique ability to question and diverge from what is—and then to create something that has never before existed—resides primarily within the domain of humanity. The gifts of diverse artistic expression, societal development, and technological innovation all result from the ability to question, and to conceive of things beyond the status quo.

Clinging to a currently accepted practice versus being curious about change and looking for alternatives are two very different ways of dealing with circumstances. Adherence begets consistency and maybe stability; questioning, searching, and discovering innovative alternatives, which is the basis of creativity, leads to change and often, advancement.

Change, though, is not always desired. In 1632, Galileo published the *Dialogue Concerning the Two Chief World Systems*, providing support for Copernicus's heliocentric theory of planetary motion. The Catholic Church condemned Galileo's work because, in the Church's view, it contradicted the scriptures. Galileo, one of the most brilliant and creative scientists in the history of humankind, was tried for heresy by the Inquisition, ordered to recant, and spent the rest of his life under house arrest. Finally, in 1992, Pope John Paul II declared that the ruling against Galileo was an error resulting from "tragic mutual incomprehension."

A great many people and religious groups continue to disagree with Darwin's theory of evolution because it contradicts their interpretation of the Bible. Refusal to investigate or consider another understanding, even when it is bolstered by overwhelming scientific evidence, is nonetheless a satisfying position for some of us. In truth, adhering to religious beliefs and practices can give us a sense of stability and reassurance: we do not want to rock our world any more than we have to. And shifting our comfortable perspective from that of a loving God, of humans made in God's image, to one that permits random natural selection resulting in humans evolving from apes (or fish!), as Darwin proposed, can be unsettling or even unacceptable.

Why is it that some people are unwilling to break free from those beliefs that are contrary to sound science, or worse, from doctrine that leads to terrible acts of inhumanity? There are many possible reasons why people differ in their interpretation of authoritative texts such as the Koran and the Bible, and these differences may be genetic or alternatively based on environmental, and educational factors such as the imprinting mentioned earlier. But perhaps there is another explanation worth exploring.

## Resolving Issues: Two Very Different Approaches

Survival has always depended on sensing circumstances in the environment and having enough stored information about them so we can perform any necessary actions in a timely manner. Of course, the know-how and ability to perform any such actions adequately are likewise required. But even without a stimulus from the environment, humans can still plan and carry out preparatory actions through their ability to think about possible future events.

Many of our behaviors, such as the way we cry when sad or laugh when amused, are genetically programmed or imprinted at an early age when we observe and imitate the behaviors of our parents, teachers, and friends. Certain complex motor skills, such as hitting a tennis ball, are controlled by procedural memories. These forms of memory are often so well established that we can perform some skills without conscious awareness. Think of how we automatically hold eating utensils or ride a bicycle.

We have many interactions with others or experience different circumstances that cannot be addressed by procedural memories. Our sophisticated brains have another store of knowledge. Referred to as declarative or semantic memories, they are formed throughout our lives. They include the ability to speak and understand speech, the ability to read and write, knowledge of mathematics and the ability to calculate, as well as spatial organization and ways of finding specific locations.

Earlier we discussed a third form of storage called episodic memory. Procedural memories help us to ride a bicycle, semantic memories allow us to know what the word "bicycle" means, and episodic memories enable us to recall when and where we rode our bike and what kind of bike it was—all the "what" and "where" details of an experience.

Throughout much of our lives, we are on an automatic pilot of sorts: when confronted with problems that require action, we retrieve memories of strategies we can employ to solve these issues quickly. But life can present situations with which we have little or no experience. When that happens, we often try to apply a solution we learned from some previous, similar problem. Fortunately, our brains are sophisticated enough not only to store memories but also to manipulate them—to reason. Reasoning makes us pretty good problem solvers. Sometimes, and to varying degrees, it works.

But what happens when memories and reasoning do not allow us to solve a problem, and a new approach or another solution is needed? Before we can take action, we need to do two things. We have to disengage from the belief that a previously used strategy will be successful, and we need to develop a new strategy.

We might want to think about these simple but sometimes very challenging actions. If we fail to disengage, what are we doing? We are adhering to a given belief and repeating an unsuccessful strategy. Although it is important to persevere until an objective is reached, continuing to do so without making progress is not only unproductive but may be abnormal.

Once an individual realizes that a particular approach is not working, and provided that she has some level of commitment to finding a solution, then, by observation and reasoning, she might conceive of another strategy. This thought process can occur through two very distinct ways of thinking: convergent and divergent reasoning.

When we are confronted with a problem for which our current solution is inadequate, then—like Copernicus, who was not satisfied with the notion of a geocentric universe—we can diverge from the status quo and imagine new possibilities. William James, a physician, philosopher, and founder of modern psychology, authored the classic textbook *Principles of Psychology* in 1890. He wrote the following about the concept of divergent reasoning:

> Instead of thoughts of concrete things patiently following one another in a beaten track of habitual suggestion, we have the most abrupt cross-cuts and transitions from one idea to another . . . unheard of combinations of elements, the subtlest associations of analogy. . . . [W]e seem suddenly introduced into a seething caldron of ideas . . . where partnerships can be joined or loosened. . . . [T]readmill routine is unknown and the unexpected is the only law.

When we apply divergent reasoning, we are open to new possibilities, especially when the current solution is not good enough. To evaluate a person's ability to disengage and use divergent reasoning, clinicians and investigators often resort to the Wisconsin Card Sorting Test. In this assessment, the test-taker develops a strategy to sort cards, but the examiner requires the subject to periodically change sorting strategies. The examiner measures the number of sorts required by the subject to find the new correct sorting strategy (such as switch from shape to color) or, in other words, disengaging from the prior sorting strategy, and using divergent reasoning to find a new strategy.

Ken occasionally employs the Alternative Uses Test, devised by the psychologist Joy Paul Guilford, to assess divergent reasoning. The patient is given a word such as *brick* and is asked to list all of its possible uses in a limited. The patient is told that the more unusual (but still practical) the proposed use, the higher the score. In this case, if the patient suggests that a brick can be used to build houses, fences, and fireplaces, he would receive a point for each suggestion. However, if somewhat more creative answers—such as bookcases, door stops, bookends, or paperweights—are offered, they might be awarded two points each. If the patient suggests breaking the brick into smaller pieces and using it as chalk or for rubbing off calluses, three points could be merited, because these latter responses demonstrate a greater degree of divergent reasoning.

When divergent reasoning is employed, information from unrelated memories or knowledge is somehow connected to arrive at a novel approach. In the example above, we would have to recall our memories about how rough a brick feels when we rub our fingers across it or maybe even get a bit of skin burn from it. Then we might think about how else we could use this abrading feature, perhaps remembering that calluses can be smoothed. Maybe we have seen someone do this, or we saw an advertisement for a similar product. Now cognizant of these two disparate pieces of information, our mind would need to draw them together into some novel combination: Aha! Break the brick into a hand-sized implement and use its rough surface to rub off a callus.

### An Example from Medicine

This divergent thought process is the opposite of what happens with convergent reasoning. A good example of convergent thinking comes from Sir Arthur Conan Doyle's Sherlock Homes. Holmes was a genius at convergent thinking, but the credit is due to his creator, Doyle. A medical doctor as well as a writer, he was taught, as are all physicians, that a diverse set of symptoms might have a single cause. On observing a series of symptoms, physicians are trained to arrive at a specific (and, when possible, a single) diagnosis. For example, if a patient presents with a momentary loss of vision in the left eye and then several hours later loses the ability to speak and develops right arm weakness, an attending neurologist might think about how these three symptoms are connected. The convergent thinking might go a little like this: The left cerebral cortex is important for speech and control of the right arm, but it is not responsible for all the vision in the left eye. Combining what she knows, the neurologist would consider how both the left eye and the left cerebral cortex receive their blood supply from the left carotid artery; this might indicate inadequate blood flow in this major artery of the neck. Perhaps, then, she might wonder if the patient's symptoms are a result of severe atherosclerosis and a blood clot in the carotid. After this bit of (well-trained) convergent reasoning, she would want this patient's carotid investigated immediately.

In the early 1950s, physicians using convergent reasoning learned that carotid atherosclerosis and blood-clot formation can obstruct blood flow, which can lead to a stroke. They also noted that, many times before patients had strokes, a few warning signs—ischemic attacks—lasting just minutes, could occur. They wondered, should such an attack be evident, would it be best to remove a potential clot immediately and perhaps prevent a stroke?

In 1958, Michael DeBakey, a surgeon in Houston, Texas, partly resolved the question by successfully performing such surgery. Fifty years later, carotid endarterectomies, as they are called, remain one of the most important means of preventing major disabling strokes. We have learned, however, that not all the expected warning signs point to carotid atherosclerosis. Some patients have atherosclerosis of arteries in the head. Sometimes blood clots migrate from the heart to the brain. Moreover, certain individuals simply are too sick from other diseases to have this surgery. Carotid endarterectomies were not, and are not, a panacea; alternatives were still needed. Would divergent reasoning provide new solutions?

Before any of these breakthroughs, in 1916, a Johns Hopkins medical student named Jay McLean was investigating, under the guidance of William Henry Howell, compounds that helped blood to coagulate. McLean stumbled on a molecule found in canine livers that, contrary to the focus of his study, had anticoagulant properties; Howell would later name it heparin. Not until the 1930s was it put to use as a treatment for abnormal clotting in veins.

In completely separate work, another compound, originally arising out of research into hemorrhaging cattle, was developed as a pesticide for rodents in the early 1940s. The compound was named warfarin. No one had a clue about using it as an anticoagulant for people—until research was triggered by its use in an unsuccessful suicide attempt. (The victim took "rat poison.") Ultimately it was approved for use as an anticoagulant. Many of us know of it today by the brand name Coumadin.

Researchers working on stoke prevention assembled all of this unrelated medical information, including that about the anticoagulants, to undertake new studies. Did these new ideas help prevent strokes? Yes and no. Heparin was found not to be helpful; warfarin is best for preventing clots when they originate from the heart. Drugs such as clopidogrel, persantine, and even aspirin turned out to be effective treatments when clots migrated from the carotid artery or other vessels that feed blood to the brain in patients who are not good surgical candidates.

Think about the disengagement from existing conditions and the curiosity about new approaches that occurred throughout this long sequence of events. Such thoughts—what is really causing these strokes, there's got to be a way to prevent them, could surgery work, could we break up or prevent arterial clots, could this compound have the desired effect, what is causing cattle to hemorrhage, there's got to be a better means of killing rats, could we use this in humans—involve divergent reasoning, and represent the kind of questioning and wondering that begins the creative process.

Creativity requires combining unrelated pieces of information to form alternative methods and ideas not previously considered. After Dr. DeBakey disengaged from the notion that doctors could do little to prevent strokes, he decided to pioneer the untested surgery. But researchers had to give up the idea that such procedures, despite their limitations, were the only choice; they had to consider other means. Throughout this process, who would have thought that, ultimately, taking a pill would be one such solution?

The final step in the creative process is verifying our reasoning by making, doing, or testing the thing we have conceived. The notion of treating potential stroke victims with precautionary surgery had to be tried. Anticoagulant compounds had to be manufactured under strict guidelines, run through a long series of animal and human clinical trials, and eventually approved for use in humans by the U.S. Food and Drug Administration.

Creativity, it has been said, is finding unity in what appears to be diversity. A previously hidden association between stroke patients and anticoagulants became apparent from this process; we now see how they join to benefit people. Even the world's most famous theoretical physics formula finds unity in what was thought to be diversity. Energy and matter, once considered separate and distinct, are now shown to be related as $E = mc^2$. In his book *Creativity and the Brain*, Heilman defines creativity as the "ability to understand, develop and express in a systematic fashion, novel orderly relationships" (2005, 154).

Although the foregoing examples have concerned the sciences, these same processes occur in many other domains. Diverging from the customary, the impressionists were the first artists to note that the beauty of a painting is not always directly related to how accurately the objects being portrayed are rendered. Popular music has continuously emerged from big band swing, ballads, rhythm and blues, rock and roll, disco, and hip-hop. Creativity occurs in nearly unlimited forms.

In our homes and at work, we may be confronted with situations that cannot be adequately addressed by old solutions. Disengaging from these old beliefs and behaviors to contemplate and attempt new things is the creative approach. Shopping, cooking, and planning a career move all can involve innovation. But what about our approach to the divine, our understanding of scriptures, or our interpretation of what our religious leaders say to us? Are we curious? Do we question? Do we look for threads that unite disparate kinds of information to arrive at our own, new conclusions?

Why are some people more willing to reason divergently, whereas others are reluctant to do so, sometimes even seeming stuck? The answer might relate to how specific areas of the brain are utilized—or not.

## It's the Frontal Lobes!

In an earlier chapter, we described how the frontal lobes allow people to disengage from physical and mental activities and how they enable the pursuit of goal-oriented actions. We noted that people with frontal-lobe damage or dysfunction often display a grasp reflex or mitgehen ("go with") such that when they see or feel the examiner's hand, they will take hold of it and not let go, or they will follow it. Individuals with even more severe frontal-lobe dysfunction will reflexively reach for, touch, and hold on to objects they see. These are termed physically adherent behaviors.

The Wisconsin Card Sort can show that some patients, especially those with injury to their frontal lobes, continue to use the same strategy repeatedly, even in the face of negative feedback from the examiner. Such perseverative behavior is typically associated with injury to the frontal lobes.

The Harvard University neurologist Derek Denny-Brown, along with Richard Chambers, demonstrated some 55 years ago that animals and patients with injured frontal lobes will inappropriately reach for and grasp things and then have trouble letting go.

In 1984, Brenda Milner and her coworkers tested patients who had portions of their frontal lobes removed for the treatment of medically intractable epilepsy by having them perform the Wisconsin Card Sorting Test. Many could make the initial sort correctly, for example, by color. However, unlike uninjured people, the participants had difficulty in disengaging from an incorrect strategy and trying new ones. Even when presented with explicit information that their method was no longer correct, they displayed this cognitive adherence.

Using functional imaging, Karen Faith Berman and colleagues at the National Institute of Mental Health studied unimpaired individuals while they performed the Wisconsin Card Sorting Test. An increase in their frontal-lobe activity during the test provided more converging evidence that this part of the brain plays an important role in the ability to disengage and reason divergently.

One of the best tests for assessing a person's ability to use divergent reasoning, as we have mentioned, is the Guilford Alternative Uses Test. The test subject is asked to suggest alternative uses for a common object (as in our earlier brick example). Using functional imaging, Carlsson and coworkers at Lund University demonstrated that individuals who produced the most divergent responses had more frontal-lobe activity than those who adhered to the normal uses of a brick.

Is the practice of strict religious fundamentalism, in which beliefs are tightly held no matter what the circumstances, a mental equivalent of physical grasping behavior? Do religious extremism and unconditional adherence to religious doctrine result from a failure of a portion of the frontal lobe to develop fully or, if it is fully developed, to activate?

## The Unconditional Adherence to Religious Fundamentalism

Enrique was just a year old when his family left Castro's Cuba and came ashore in Florida. He grew up Catholic, but was exposed to Santería, a religion where African beliefs and practices are tied together with those of the Roman Catholic Church, so perhaps this mixture of religions allowed him some flexibility about religious and spiritual beliefs. Eventually he matured into a somewhat conservative adult and today is successful in his real estate business. In his midlife, though, feeling drawn to learning more about God, Enrique signed up for Bible study classes. He was looking forward to sharing and discussing the meaning of scripture with the group and gaining some deeper insights into life. That enthusiasm quickly faded. When he would ponder, out loud, if there was some other meaning to the Virgin birth story, for example, he was told to not wonder about such things: "Just read the scripture—everything you need to know is right there; don't read into it. And don't use your imagination. That's already been done for you and written into the Word." Enrique was admonished to stick to the literal text.

Religious fundamentalists, by definition, strongly adhere to religious doctrine. Divergence from holy writings, including personal interpretation, is not well tolerated. An American Public Media special, "The Power of Fundamentalism," reporting on three reformed fundamentalists—one representing Christianity; another, Judaism; and the third, Islam—who said, in essence, that they were taught to believe as they were told, that personal interpretation and imagination were unwanted; adherence to doctrine was essential.[1]

A Christian Web site reads: "Scripture is the believer's sufficient guide for all of faith and practice, and Christians must believe and obey whatever it teaches and commands. The Bible provides the Christian—through precept, pattern and principle—all that is necessary to make wise decisions concerning the many ethically complex issues of life (2 Tim. 3:16–17; 2 Pet. 1:3); and educational methodology is not neutral. The Christian should build his educational methodology from the word of God and reject methodologies derived from humanism, evolutionism, and other unbiblical systems of thought."[2]

A 2012 Gallup poll showed that 67 percent of Americans who attend church regularly believe that God created humans, as they look today, within the last 10,000 years.[3] Christian fundamentalists regularly attempt to ban the teaching of evolution in public schools. Their current strategy is to have the biblical perspective of creationism taught in science class alongside evolution.

In 1974, a disagreement over the choice of school textbooks became violent, with shootings and even dynamite, when a West Virginia county school board, locals, and Christians clashed. Those who supported the board's selection of textbooks, as the account goes, "generally believed that, in an increasingly global society with interconnected economies, students needed to have access to the languages and ideas of diverse cultures." This included an obligation to challenge existing belief systems as well as to question the U.S. government. What kinds of books could so raise the ire of the involved Christians that some would resort to shooting and setting explosives? Those by the poet Allen Ginsberg, the black rights advocate Eldridge Cleaver, and Sigmund Freud, as well as George Orwell's *Animal Farm* and *The Autobiography of Malcolm X*. A protest sign read: "I have a Bible I don't need those dirty books."[4]

Certainly fundamentalists adhere to many beliefs and practices that are not injurious, not demeaning, and not intolerant of others. Feeling the need to pray and worship regularly, reflecting on the moral standards set forth by God in view of their own personal actions, and concern and help for the needy are activities that can engender stability in families and societies. Religion can bring great comfort and peace to those with faith. These outcomes are not to be taken lightly.

But when our actions fly squarely in the face of sound science, or worse, we conduct terrible acts of inhumanity in the name of God, as was discussed in Chapter 7, might these actions be displays of a compulsive adherence disorder? If so, such actions may indeed have a partially biological explanation: a reduced utilization of the most phylogenetically evolved part of the brain, the part that plays a vital role in our ability to reason divergently and be creative—the frontal lobes.

Something is puzzling, though. People who unconditionally adhere to religious doctrine can have a high intelligence quotient (IQ) and certainly can be as smart as the next person. If a vital and evolved portion of their brain is being underutilized, how can this be?

## Creative Genius and Religious Fundamentalism

Several years ago, *Commentary* magazine published an article titled "Jewish Genius." Charles Murray, who makes it clear that he is not Jewish, attempts to explain the extravagant overrepresentation of Jews, relative to their numbers, in the top ranks of the arts, sciences, law, medicine, finance, entrepreneurship, and the media. He notes, for example, that Jews make up only two-tenths of 1 percent of the world's population, but in the second half of the twentieth century, they received 29 percent of the Nobel prizes awarded. So far, in the twenty-first century, they have received 32 percent of the Nobel prizes. His explanation for this disproportionate success in the arts and creative sciences is relatively simple: Jews, in general, are just smarter or more highly intelligent than other people. But how important is "intelligence" in such innovative and creative endeavors? And, if it is not intelligence, what is the essential factor?

Modern intelligence testing was first introduced in France in the early twentieth century. The French government was aware that some children learned faster than others and therefore wanted them tested for appropriate class placement. Alfred Binet, who was primarily responsible for developing this test, found that, in general, the older the child the higher his or her score. As a result, he was able to determine an average score for each age group. The term *intelligence quotient* is derived from the means by which a youngster's score was determined: dividing his or her mental age, as determined by the score on this test, by the average score of other children the same age and multiplying the result by 100. For example, if a child got the same score as the mean of his age group, he would have a ratio of 1; when that ratio was multiplied by 100, his IQ would be 100. If his score was very high, meaning that he performed like someone much older than his chronological age, he would have a high IQ. A score above 130 or 140 often rates the label "genius."

A psychologist at Stanford University named Lewis Terman modified Binet's test and created what became the American standard for IQ testing: The Stanford-Binet intelligence test. Terman was fascinated by human intelligence and wanted to understand how the high intelligence of youngsters whose IQ testing placed them at genius level would affect their lives. Systematically following a large group of kids with very high IQs, known as "Terman's geniuses," he learned that, as adults, most had very successful careers. However, not one of Terman's geniuses was awarded a Nobel Prize, and none were even considered creative geniuses by historians. There were, however, two other children we should note.

As children, William Shockley and Luís Alvarez did not score high enough on their IQ tests to be included in Terman's geniuses. Shockley went on to invent the transistor and received a Nobel Prize for his remarkable scientific advance. Alvarez was responsible for inventing three important radar systems used during World War II, as well as helping to develop the detonators used to set off the plutonium bomb. He also made a number of important discoveries in optics and cosmic rays. Alvarez also received a Nobel Prize. These guys were creative geniuses, but not a Terman, or IQ, genius.

A reasonable IQ is, of course, necessary for creativity. A person must have sufficient knowledge and skill to develop an innovative idea. The physicians who developed the treatments for stroke had to have had extensive knowledge about anatomy, physiology, and pathology (especially of the circulatory, hematological, and nervous systems). Likewise, artists must be familiar with color mixing and medium application processes and must have the skill to create representations. Any creative endeavor works this way.

Many of us, along with most psychologists, have viewed the ability to acquire and use knowledge and skills for problem solving as a measure of IQ. And that is indeed what IQ tests measure: they usually do not assess divergent reasoning. On the face of it, this sounds completely logical. People with very high IQs have been labeled geniuses, with the implication that creative geniuses are IQ geniuses. But that is not necessarily the case.

Without question, creativity and intelligence are related. But their association is, perhaps, not quite what we might expect. In his book *Origins of Genius*, Dean Simonton reviews the evidence that an IQ threshold does exist: above an IQ of approximately 120, IQ no longer predicts a person's creative abilities; IQ and creativity then become disassociated. This means that a person can be a genius as measured by his or her IQ, yet not be as creative as another person with a lower IQ. Knowing this, we need to reframe our formerly accepted opinions about intelligence and what being smart may really encompass.

In his bestselling book *Emotional Intelligence*, Daniel Goleman introduces us to something he refers to as emotional intelligence. (He calls it EQ.) He claims it is distinct from and perhaps more important for our personal success and happiness than IQ. We suggest that there is yet another way of being smart—a creative intelligence (CR)—and that CR is different from both IQ and EQ, and perhaps every bit as important.

Does it really make sense that someone can have high intelligence of one kind but not another? A good example of the dissociation between emotional intelligence and IQ comes from the fabulous movie *Forrest Gump*. Forrest has a low IQ but is gifted with a relatively high level of emotional intelligence. In contrast, Jenny, the love of Forrest's life, appeared to suffer from what psychiatrists call a borderline personality disorder, as well as a reduced level of emotional intelligence. Despite Forrest's low IQ, his life is relatively fulfilling. In contrast, Jenny's higher IQ but lower emotional intelligence caused her to have a miserable life and a tragic death. In a similar way, Terman's exclusion of Alvarez and Shockley from his group of geniuses showed the dissociation between intelligence, as measured by IQ tests, and the ability to be creative.

So although in his *Commentary* article, Charles Murray says the disproportionate number of Jews who are Nobel laureates is due to their high IQ, we suggest something else: It is a result of creative intelligence—and the divergent reasoning from which it bloomed.

But why Jews? We do not know for sure. What we do know is that creative success absolutely relies on the ability to question, doubt, and search for new alternatives. Copernicus, Galileo, Darwin, and Martin Luther all did it. So did the scientists and physicians involved with preventing strokes. That first essential step of doubting and questioning the status quo is a kind of disobedience, is it not? I *don't believe in this. I am not going to do this anymore. I want to find a new way.* Does the preponderance of successful Jews arise from a propensity for such disobedience?

Except for the Jewish New Year, Rosh Hashanah, and the Day of Atonement, Yom Kippur, most of the Jewish holidays, such as Passover, Purim, and Chanukah, celebrate the Jews' victory over tyrannical regimes or deliverance from inhumane conquerors. The revolts usually started because the Jews were disobedient and did not follow their tyrants' dictums.

In addition to celebrating these feats of disobedience and success, almost all Jewish children are told the story of what Abraham, considered the founder of Judaism, did as a child in his father's store. His father was a merchant who sold statuary idols to his Mesopotamian customers. As a young child, Abraham had the realization that idol worship was foolish. (He questioned and doubted.) One day, while watching the store, he used a hammer to smash all the idols except for the largest one. He then put the hammer in the remaining statue's hands. When his father returned, he saw all the smashed statues. Stunned, he asked Abraham what had happened. Abraham pointed to the large idol with the hammer and explained that they got into a fight and the biggest one destroyed all the others. Hearing this, his father told him, "Do not be silly. Those idols cannot do anything." The moral of this story, taught to almost all Jewish children, is that disobedience in the pursuit of truth and justice is not only justified but also is desirable and necessary.

During Jewish rituals such as the Passover Seder, part of the service involves having children ask questions. For example, the youngest child at this dinner service asks four questions, starting with, "Why is this night different from all other nights?" Children who are raised in an environment that consistently encourages questioning and rewards divergent reasoning have a greater likelihood of growing up to be creative adults. Is such nurturing a partial explanation for Jewish success in Nobel awards? Perhaps.

When we look back at those who have been very creative over the last fifty years, such as the Nobel Prize winners, it is difficult to find laureates who were religious fundamentalists. The child who declares, "I do not believe in this; I want another answer" or "There must be another way" would be considered disobedient by authoritative parents. When portions of the brain are stimulated they become better developed. For example, children who are trained to play musical instruments have a larger auditory cortex than children who do not learn to play instruments. Therefore, parents who encourage or demand strict adherence to religious beliefs and punish divergent reasoning could impair the development of portions of the child's frontal lobes. Although not formally researched, children brought up in this environment may have a higher probability of growing into adults who are susceptible to adherence behaviors and who eschew divergent reasoning.

American universities have become major sources of innovation, from medicine to clean technology to social science. Yet Christian fundamentalist leaders such as the late Jerry Falwell, Sr. and Pat Robertson have expressed concern about the many ostensibly agnostic, atheist, and/or liberal faculty members who mentor students at America's leading research universities. In addition, students at secular universities are not required to attend religious services or follow religious guidelines. Because of their concerns about modern universities not educating their students in fundamentalist thinking, Falwell and Robertson founded their own universities. These universities, however, have not been bastions of creative productivity in either the sciences or the arts.

Some of world's greatest scientists are members of the National Academy of Sciences. As we mentioned earlier, Edward J. Larson and Larry Witham conducted a survey of all the members who were either biological or physical scientists. They found that 72.2 percent were atheists, 20.8 percent were agnostic, and only 7 percent believed in God.

In this survey the investigators did not mention the religion of these scientists' parents. We have to be careful not to sound as if we were promoting Jews as a superior class of people, because we absolutely are not. But we are confident in saying that the success of Jews in creative endeavors related to Nobel Prizes, science, medicine, the arts, business, and other professions may be more a function of a questioning mentality that leads to divergent reasoning and creative intelligence, rather than IQ. Thus, if a child is born to a Jewish mother, the child is considered a Jew. Judaism is more than a religion: it is also a culture in which humanism plays a critical role. Many Jews are secular, with agnostic or atheistic beliefs. But religious beliefs may be less important than the propensity for questioning and seeking alternatives, and Jews certainly do not have a monopoly on the ability to question. Is it not incumbent on all peoples to raise their children so that they too learn to question and seek new answers? We are not suggesting the cultivation of insolence, but rather, the promotion of divergent reasoning and creativity that may lead to a better life for humankind.

## Notes

1. "The Power of Fundamentalism," *On Being with Krista Tippett*, American Public Media, August 19, 2004, http://www.onbeing.org/program/power-fundamentalism/218
2. "The Tenets of Biblical Patriarchy," Vision Forum Ministries, San Antonio, TX Copyright © 2001–2013 Vision Forum Ministries,® http://www.visionforumministries.org/home/about/biblical_patriarchy.aspx
3. Frank Newport, "In U.S., 46% Hold Creationist View of Human Origins," Gallup, June 1, 2012, http://www.gallup.com/poll/155003/hold-creationist-view-human-origins.aspx
4. Trey Kay, Deborah George, and Stan Bumgardner, "The Great Textbook War," *American RadioWorks*, American Public Media, 2009, http://americanradioworks.publicradio.org/features/textbooks/

# 9   Our Spirituality
## Beyond You

*The most beautiful and most profound emotion we can experience is the sensa-tion of the mystical. It is the sower of all true science. So to whom this emotion is a stranger, who can no longer wonder and stand rapt in awe, is as good as dead. To know that which is impenetrable to us really exists, manifesting itself as the highest wisdom and the most radiant beauty which our dull faculties can comprehend only in their primitive forms—this knowledge, this feeling is at the centre of true religiousness.*

—Albert Einstein—The Merging of Spirit and Science

## The Experience Beyond Things

The meaning of the word *spirituality* cannot be fully explained by a brief and simple definition. Merriam-Webster's Dictionary says it is "having a spiritual meaning or reality that is not apparent to the senses." We may understand it as a personal intuition and experience of the divine that transcends our ordinary understanding of things. Reading the quote by Einstein above, we might see his use of the term *mystical* as referring to a belief in some reality beyond our five senses. And spirituality could include accepting the notion that life has a meaning that transcends our corporeal world.

According to the *Dictionary of Philosophy* by Peter Adam Angeles, the mys-tical experience itself, and the knowledge thereby gained from this experience can never be full described or conceptualized. However, there are several char-acteristics, including an intense and important, but transient life experience that bring feelings of joy or serenity and a sense of oneness and unity. This experi-ence can be brought about by meditation and contemplation, as well as ascetic practices and drugs.

In contrast to spirituality, religiosity carries a more pointed definition—the belief in and practice of a specific system of doctrines shared by a group of people and defined by prescribed rules, value systems, dogma, and prac-tices. Why does it seem so challenging to craft a succinct definition for spirituality?

Ken's granddaughter, Ashton, was seven when she first questioned him about electricity. "What is it, Pop-Pop?" she asked. "It is a kind of energy carried in wires," he replied, trying to be informative. But that answer did not help much, because she then asked, "What's energy?"

"Well, there are different kinds of energy," Ken said. "Some you can feel and, some you can see. Light is an energy we can see. Heat is a kind we can feel. When we jump in the air, we can feel the energy of gravity pulling us down, right? And when we get two magnets close together we can feel them push or pull—which is magnetic energy. So, energy is not something with weight and shape that we can pick up or drop, but it can give us comfort like warmth, make stuff happen, like moving things and giving us light so we can see."

Ken mused over his response to his granddaughter and began thinking about an analogy between energy and spirituality: some of us can sense a divine presence. It has power, it is invisible, and it is unlike any strictly physical object. Just like the various forms of energy, the experience of spirituality and the mystical may come to us in different ways.

Albert Einstein wrote an essay called "Cosmic Religion," which was published in the *New York Times Magazine* on November 9, 1930. Einstein wrote about three levels of religion—that of fear, with a God who protects, rewards and punishes; a second related to morality, like that of the Ten Commandments; and a third level he called the "cosmic religious sense." Einstein explained that, unlike an anthropomorphic concept of God, here, at this third level, a person feels the nobility and marvelous order revealed in nature and in the world of thought. The person feels that individual destiny is a form of imprisonment and seeks to experience the totality of existence as a unity full of significance.

We might define Einstein's third level as spirituality. But how do humans go about feeling or experiencing the order revealed in nature or the totality of existence as a unity? Einstein did not rely on traditional religious beliefs. He wrote, "I do not believe in a personal God. If something is in me which can be called religious, then it is the unbounded admiration for the structure of the world so far as our science can reveal it" (Dawkins, 2006, 36). And, another often cited quote taken from *The Private Albert Einstein*, by Peter Bucky and Alan Weakland, is, "The most beautiful and most profound emotion we can experience is the sensation of the mystical" (1992, p. 86).

In an earlier chapter, we discussed the concept of agent, or agency, as the something out there that has intention, the something that causes a thing to happen. As children develop a sense of this agency, they also begin to recognize the self. They learn that their actions can cause things to happen, independent of their parents and siblings. This early awareness, or mastery, of agency can provide kids with a sense of pleasure. We have all seen youngsters in their high chairs intentionally dropping food on the floor, mastering their sense of control right in the face Mom and Dad's disapproval.

We might not see it this way and, surely, the parents cleaning up the mess on the floor will not, but this child's actions are the beginning of goal-oriented behavior. It sounds laughable, but think about this: in order to make plans and set goals, we have to have a clear sense of self—in other words, an awareness of our self that can independently act and alter our environment.

Such awareness of independence, though, has a down side. When children learn they can act as self-determining agents, they also begin to realize that their parents can do the same. But here is the twist. Early in life, we have neither sense of self nor knowledge of independence. The converse, unity, reigns: an awareness of unity with Mom, Dad, and everything else. Where did that go? And how might we regain it if we wanted to? We would say, through the temporary abandonment of our sense of self. Doing that means we must reduce the activity of certain areas in the brain, those that mediate agency and activate goal-oriented behaviors—the frontal lobes.

## The Frontal Lobes Again: Seeing What's Not There

Our frontal lobes are composed of three major anatomical subdivisions. One is on the side (the lateral,), another on the bottom (the orbitofrontal), and a third in the middle (the medial). Each of these subdivisions has different neural connections and distinct functions. The orbitofrontal portion has an important influence on and helps to control emotions (the emotional executive). The lateral portion is important in determining how best to interact with items that we see, hear, and feel (the environmental executive). This lateral portion of the frontal lobe allows us to decide when to act in response to these stimuli and what actions we should take. It also prevents us from performing actions that are meaningless or even harmful. In contrast, the medial portion of the frontal lobes allows to us initiate or inhibit goal-directed actions even in the absence of external stimuli (the self-executive).

We have learned the functions of these regions from studying animals and humans who have injury to these portions of the frontal lobes. In contrast to people with lateral-frontal-lobe damage, who can interact inappropriately with their environment, those with medial-frontal injury are impaired at initiating spontaneous behaviors without some form of external stimulus. For example, after a stroke that damages both the left and right medial frontal lobes, an individual may not be able to speak spontaneously but will repeat the words spoken by another. They will not spontaneously initiate actions important for their self-care, including personal hygiene, nor will they take care of family members, their pets, or their living quarters. However, strong internal stimuli such as hunger may prompt them to initiate action.

Prayer rituals often involve interacting with external stimuli. We look at religious images, or iconography, and hold prayer beads to help induce an appropriate state of mind. Sometimes such symbols can inspire this mental state with little or no conscious effort by the observer. In other kinds of meditation and invocation, a person might focus attention internally on words quietly repeated or images held in the mind. For example, a mantra, a word without specific meaning, is repeated silently to help engender a sense of transcendence. Because the mind is preoccupied with this repetitive activity, the person meditating is less aware of external events and not so likely to think about chores and other mundane activities. During prayer time, most of us will sit quietly alone, with our eyes closed, shutting off the outside world.

Jim Austin, the author of *Zen and the Brain*, says that this form of meditation is "top down," meaning the meditator is generating his or her own internal stimuli. Although this might seem puzzling at first, Austin suggested to Ken that some meditations involve an opposite approach: endeavoring to reach a heightened awareness of, or saturation with, the immediate environment. There is no top-down programming in these forms of meditation. Using this method, people may find they can mentally move beyond a personal sense of self and extend out into their surroundings and develop the experience of unity.

### Not Seeing Can Lead to Believing

Spiritual visionaries often seem to have histories of transformational spiritual experiences, events that forever altered their lives. Despite differences in belief systems, an interesting common thread runs through a number of these experiences: sensory isolation.

Around the age of 40, and very unhappy with his life in Mecca, Muhammad retreated to a cave in the surrounding mountains. While isolated there and in a state of profound reflection and meditation, he received his initial revelation from Allah.

The founder of the Society of Jesus (Jesuit Order), Ignatius Loyola, was born in 1491 in northern Spain. At the age of 16 he served as a page for the treasurer of the kingdom of Castile. At the wealthy court, he developed a taste for women, gambling, and swordplay. He later became a military officer. While defending the fortress at Pamplona against the French, he was struck by a cannonball that broke one of his legs and injured the other. Anesthesia was nonexistent. The physicians did their best to set the fracture, but it did not heal properly and had to be broken again. The attempt was unsuccessful. Even after further procedures, his leg remained misshapen.

Later, when traveling to Barcelona, Ignatius came across a cave near the river Cardoner and ended up living there for almost a year. It was here that he developed his *Spiritual Exercises*. Ignatius said he had visions that led him to enlightenment and resulted in the principles that became the foundation of Jesuit spirituality.

The Greek word for "single" or "solitary" is *monarchos*, from which the word *monk* is derived. The monastic life is, of course, one of solitude. It would seem that the more one is influenced or captivated by external sensory stimuli, the more difficult it can be to have the kind of experiences in which the sense of self dissolves in communion with the divine. Some indirect support for this idea may come from the field of medicine. We have known that the loss of sensation can induce hallucinations. When both eyes require surgery, for example, ophthalmologists typically will operate on one at a time; only after the first eye recovers will they proceed to the other eye. They do this because they know that if both eyes are bandaged and covered after surgery, the patient might experience visual hallucinations. This phenomenon was originally reported in the eighteenth century by the Swiss scientist Charles Bonnet, who noted that his grandfather, with impaired vision from cataracts, was having hallucinations. Today, this symptom is known as Charles Bonnet syndrome.

This hallucination phenomenon also occurs with other parts of the body and in other sensory systems. When a leg is amputated and can no longer provide sensory information to the brain, the patient may still feel like the leg is present. This phenomenon is called the "phantom limb." Sometimes the amputee feels as if this leg is in an unusual, even contorted, position, but cannot control this phantom limb.

During the 1960s, people who wanted to venture into the psychedelic realm without drugs could experiment with sensory deprivation. Special water-filled, sensory-isolation tanks, made popular by John Lilly, often induced such experiences. The tanks create an environment of total darkness, without sight, sound, or smell. The water is maintained at body temperature, so the immersed person feels neither warmth nor cold. Floating, motionless, the person cannot even sense the pull of gravity.

The famous Nobel Prize–winning physicist Richard Feynman met John Lilly and subsequently used the sensory isolation tank a number of times. Feynman wanted to experience hallucinations, but eschewed drugs. In his book *Surely You're Joking*, he wrote that after being in these tanks for several hours, "I had hallucinations almost every time, and I was able to move further and further outside of my body."

What Feynman underwent—the feeling of being beyond or outside one's own body—is often categorized as a spiritual experience. Why depriving the physical body of sensory stimulation causes spiritual experiences or hallucinations is not entirely clear; sensory deprivation may activate networks in the brain and induce these experiences.

The feeling of being more than just our bodies and having an awareness of things that are not actually present are in some respects hallucinations. Hallucinations share some attributes with what many of us know as imagery. Although when we use the term *imagery*, we often think of imagining or seeing things in our mind's eye, the concept of sensing something that is not present can occur in other sensory systems, such as hearing, smell, taste, and touch. Imagery is different from hallucinating in that the former is usually intentional; that is not so with hallucinating. Functional brain-imaging studies have shown that when people are hallucinating, the portions of the brain that normally would be engaged in perceiving the actual sensory stimuli are active. In other words, it is as if the individual were actually seeing, feeling, or hearing things that are not present. In order to perceive and recognize something—real or imagined—our brain must hold a memory or some mental representation of this thing. For example, if we see a family member's face, we recognize it because we have a stored memory of it (as well of countless other faces).

Studies of patients who have lost the ability to recognize familiar faces suggest that the part of the brain storing these memories is the fusiform gyrus, located in the bottom (ventral portion) of the occipital lobes (Figure 4.3). Functional imaging studies of uninjured people supports this brain localization. When we look at pictures of familiar faces, this area shows increased activation. It should be no surprise that when a healthy individual is asked simply to image someone's face, this same region becomes active.

If we are asked to perform an imagery task—for example to try to remember whether or not the former president Bill Clinton has a thin upper lip—the evidence suggests that most of us would do this by looking away or closing our eyes for a moment. If we instead try to imagine what Clinton's upper lip looks like with our eyes wide open and while looking at someone's face, the fusiform gyrus is likely to be too active processing the current (on-line) visual information to be able to activate any stored images of the former president.

If reducing stimulation (in this case, by closing our eyes or looking away) allows the activation of stored images, then perhaps without conscious intention, sensory isolation does something similar. By definition, in the absent intention, such imaginings would be hallucinations.

Here is a simple analogy of how this works. Imagine that the visual area in the back of the brain is like a computer monitor, and pretend that images can be projected onto it from two different sources—but only one at a time. The first source is a live, streaming video camera (which is analogous to our eyes); the second is a prerecorded DVD (which is like the images stored in our brains). From an evolutionary perspective, viewing the immediate environment around us in real time probably is more important to survival than recalling or imagining prior events. In humans, as in other animals, images coming from the video camera would take precedence over those from the DVD; in our Bill Clinton example, a previously stored image is more readily accessed when we pause the video camera.

From prehistory to the present, certain indigenous people have used hallucinogenic plants and fungi to induce visions that lead to mystical and spiritual experiences. More recently, LSD and psilocybin have been familiar drugs of choice, though not necessarily with spiritual intent.

Roland Griffiths, a Professor in the Departments of Psychiatry and Neuroscience at Johns Hopkins, along with his colleagues conducted a study in which they administered psilocybin to a group of subjects who reported all those things we would associate with a mystical or spiritual experience: feelings of unity, pure awareness, a merging with ultimate reality, a sense that all things are alive, all is one, and a transcendence of time and space.

Although people have used such drugs extensively for millennia, exactly how they induce what we might consider spiritual experiences remains unclear.

We know they prompt illusions and hallucinations. And although we have said that generally there is a difference between a hallucination and a spiritual experience, perceiving the presence of something not physically present, divine or otherwise, may employ similar brain mechanisms.

Neurons, you may recall, signal other neurons by emitting chemical neurotransmitters. After communicating with adjacent receptor cells, these receiving neurons will have either increased or decreased activity levels. With the use of functional imaging we know that serotonin, one of the major neurotransmitters in the human brain, has its rate of release increased by mind-altering drugs such as psilocybin and LSD.

Although we do not know entirely how these mind-altering drugs produce their effects, in a 2003 study of 15 healthy men, the clinical psychologist Jacqueline Borg and her coworkers appear to have discovered that those participants with higher serotonin production were more spiritual than those with lower production. They reported a negative correlation between serotonin autoreceptors and spirituality. Although this statement may sound contradictory, it is not. When activated, these autoreceptors actually reduce the level of serotonin produced. In other words, the subjects with fewer autoreceptors were more spiritual than those with more of them. We still do not fully know how alterations of serotonin influence spirituality, but the enhanced activity of the serotonin system may inhibit the brain from processing sensory stimuli.

According to the video analogy, when someone takes a drug such as psilocybin or LSD, the effect of the drug on the brain is like closing down the video camera. With the live streaming input turned off, stored images are activated without intention. In many respects, the experience is like that of the isolation tank or the cave used for retreat from the world so that hallucinations and mystical experiences may ensue.

Humans, like other animals, have to deal with enemies and predators as well as with family and friends. Our brains, therefore, attempt to learn the cause of any change that we detect. When we use imagery, we are aware that seeing something in the "mind's eye" is volitional and that we are the agent. Because hallucinations are not volitional, we might not be aware that we are the agent and thus attribute such visions to a divine source. The hallucinations that enhance people's religious beliefs and spiritual experiences are often called "visions."

The Book of Ezekiel, for example, tells of us of Ezekiel's visions—seeing God leave the Temple because of the abominations being practiced there, Israel's enemies being destroyed, and a new age of peace established. After peace is established, we are told that Ezekiel is transported to Jerusalem, where he sees a new nation, centered in a new Temple, where God's glory has returned. The Bible contains many other stories of visions. Isolation tanks and hallucinogenic drugs aside, spiritual experiences may be more commonplace than we know. Why? Because humanity is gifted with sophisticated frontal lobes—more developed than those of any other animal species on earth, and with that gift come unique possibilities.

### *Approach or Avoidance—Focus or Dissolution*

As we mentioned earlier, the idea that the frontal lobes play a key role in disengaging from sensory stimuli was put forth by Derek Denny-Brown and Richard Chambers more than 50 years ago. Denny-Brown and Chambers claimed that from the simplest single-celled organism to modern humans, all animals are capable of two distinct, fundamental behaviors: that of approach—going toward something—and avoidance, moving away from it.

According to Denny-Brown and Chambers, the back (posterior) part of the cerebral cortex (the posterior temporal and parietal regions) is important in approach behavior. The more forward or anterior regions, such as the frontal lobes, are key to avoidance. But both the front and back regions are substantially interconnected and can influence one another. Additionally, the frontal lobes may be capable of selectively inhibiting or activating portions of the temporal and parietal cortex. These researchers' assertion was based in part on several supporting factors. One involved animal studies in which Denny-Brown and coworkers removed different parts of the cerebral cortex in monkeys; the other involved examining patients who had injury to portions of their frontal lobes or their posterior temporal-parietal regions.

Earlier, we discussed the means by which information from the major sensory systems, including vision, hearing, and touch, are received and analyzed in the back or posterior portions of our brains (Figure 2.5 and 2.6), with each sensory receptor sending information to specific primary sensory areas in the brain (visual information to the occipital lobes, touch to the front portion of the parietal lobes, and hearing to the upper portion of the temporal lobes). The cerebral cortex performs an analysis of incoming sensory stimuli. For example, the primary auditory areas determine the amplitude (loudness) and frequency (pitch) of incoming sounds.

Each of these receiving areas then transmits this analyzed information to another part of the cerebral cortex, the modality-specific sensory-association areas. These specific sensory-association areas help to synthesize the incoming data, form a percept, and compare this percept to previously stored percepts. For example, when we listen to someone talk, the auditory association areas can form percepts of the phonemes or letter sounds that make up words, then synthesize these sounds and recognize a previously learned word.

The percepts may be further processed by being transmitted to parts of the temporal and parietal lobes, where the integration of visual, auditory, and tactile information takes place. Because these areas receive information from the different sensory systems, they are called polymodal association areas (Figure 2.6). It is in these polymodal areas that conceptual and symbolic information is processed and stored.

Here is an example of how this works. Let us say that someone says the word *cat*. The sound waves that enter our ears cause vibrations of our eardrums that our inner ears change to electrical signals. These signals travel into the brain and up to our auditory cortex. Our primary auditory cortex analyzes these signals and determines these vibrations' pitch, loudness, and duration. Our brain recognizes that these are sounds of spoken letters, *c*, *a*, and *t*. Our brain combines the auditory neural representations of these letter sounds or phonemes into a neural representation of the word sound *cat*. In the back top part of the temporal lobe on the left side of the brain is the portion of the auditory association cortex that stores the memories of previously heard words (Wernicke's area), but not their meaning. After we recognize the word *cat*, the auditory association cortex then excites polymodal areas as well as other association areas in other portions of the brain, so that we know what this creature looks and feels like and even the sounds that this creature can utter. Whereas polymodal integration allows us to interpret incoming sensory information, another polymodal area appears to plays a key role in directing our attention to—or to mentally approaching—the important stimuli in our environment.

Look at Figure 9.1 and fix your eyes on the cross hairs. While doing so, you should also be able to see the dot on the other side of the page. If you continue to stare at this cross without moving the paper, your head, or your eyes, the dot seems to fade from sight after 20 seconds or so. This reduction or loss of awareness of an environmental stimulus is referred as Troxler fading and appears to be a form of habituation. There are many examples of this habituation phenomenon. When a gentleman walks in the room, we immediately notice his cologne; but after just a few minutes, we are no longer aware of it. Similarly, we hear a sufficiently loud air conditioner come on, yet after short time, the noise fades into the background. We slip into a new pair of shoes and feel them pressing against our feet; but after we have had them on for a while, we no longer feel them.

Working with Mark Mennemeier and other co-investigators, Ken tested patients with damage to their posterior temporal and inferior parietal lobes. The researchers noticed that the patients would very quickly habituate when looking at a dot similar to that in Figure 9.1—it would fade away in short order. In contrast, a different set of patients with similar damage—but to their frontal lobes—were very slow to habituate: the dot lingered in their perception.

Mark and Ken's observations clearly showed a habituation difference between the two groups of patients, and research by others offers similar evidence. Why this happens is not fully understood.

Earlier we described how the thalamus acts as a sensory relay station, transmitting sensory information to the cortex for analysis (Figure 9.2). Surrounding this relay station is a ring of neurons (the thalamic reticular nucleus) that, when activated, may inhibit the relay of information to the cortex. We believe the normal activation of the frontal lobes may trigger this "gatekeeper" inhibiting

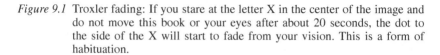

*Figure 9.1* Troxler fading: If you stare at the letter X in the center of the image and do not move this book or your eyes after about 20 seconds, the dot to the side of the X will start to fade from your vision. This is a form of habituation.

effect, so that ordinary sensory information is kept from the cerebral cortex and from the individual's awareness. We no longer smell the cologne, hear the air conditioner, or feel our new shoes. But a damaged frontal lobe is unable to trigger the gatekeeper, and the image lingers.

Unlike in frontal lobe activation, the parietal lobes work to keep the gate open so that sensory information can proceed to the cortex. The push is for the fragrance of the cologne, the sound of the air conditioner, and the feel of the shoes to linger. But that does not usually happen; where the balance is between the parietal and frontal lobes' influence over the gatekeeper remains unclear. Maybe, as mentioned above, the influence is related to the neurotransmitter serotonin. In any case, awareness likely depends on factors other than those responsible for habituation. One day when he was a young medical student, Ken was walking through the ward at the University of Virginia Hospital when someone yelled out at him, "Hey doc, can you come over here?"

Ken obliged and asked how he could help. The patient, Hank, down at his food tray and asked, "Why do they only serve vegetables around here?"

Ken looked at Hank's plate and noticed he had eaten all of the vegetables from the right side of the plate, but the fried chicken on the left side was untouched. "You have chicken on your plate," Ken said. Still, Hank said he could not see it. As a medical student, Ken had learned that if someone has a stroke to the occipital lobe on one side of the brain, the damage could limit his or her ability to see the entire space in front of them. This loss of vision usually occurs in the visual space opposite the side of the injury. Being beside Hank, Ken also noticed that he had some weakness of his left arm. Thinking about this kind of stroke condition, Ken turned Hank's plate around 180 degrees; the chicken was now in the opposite visual field. That did the trick, and Hank immediately thanked him for the fried chicken. Ken stayed with him for a while and tried something else. Facing Hank, he moved his own right hand, which was in Hank's left visual field of vision, the same side as the chicken on Hank's plate. Ken noticed that Hank had no trouble seeing his moving hand. But why he could not see the food on the left side of his plate was still a puzzle.

The next day, as Ken was walking by Hank's bed, Hank called out again. This time, he was looking down at his left arm. He picked it up with his other hand, and said, "Doc, can you get this man out of my bed?"

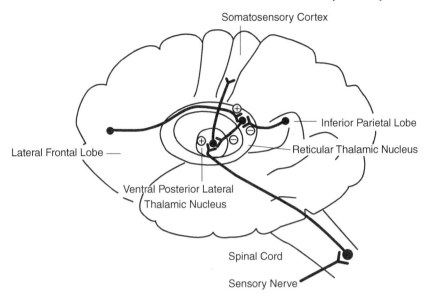

*Figure 9.2* Thalamic sensory gating: Sensory information coming from the eyes, ears, and skin is sent by nerves to the thalamus, which relays this information to the primary sensory cortical areas (Figure 2.6). This drawing of the thalamus shows the somatosensory thalamic nucleus that relays tactile stimuli. The thalamus has different nuclei; the one that relays touch on the body is the ventral posterior lateral nucleus. Surrounding this nucleus is another thalamic nucleus called the thalamic reticular nucleus. Plus signs indicate an excitatory influence; minus signs, inhibitory influence. When the thalamic reticular nucleus is active it prevents or inhibits information from being relayed to the cortex. The frontal lobes appear to activate (help close) this gate; the parietal lobes inhibit (open) this gate.

Ken tried to convince him that it was his own arm, but to no avail. Hank then attempted to throw his left arm out of bed, but it snapped back and hit him in his chest.

After doing some research into these symptoms, Ken realized that patients like Hank do not have a loss of sensory input, but rather a profound attention disorder called the neglect syndrome. They can be unaware of objects on one side of space and stimuli applied to one side of their bodies.

Hank and the many other patients like him suffer from an injury to their right inferior parietal lobe. The reason that this region is so important for mediating attention to both a person's surrounding environment and their body is not entirely known. We do know, though, that this is a polymodal area; not only do the visual, auditory, and tactile sensory-association areas converge here, but information also arrives from the limbic system, important in determining the emotional significance of stimuli, and from the portions of the frontal lobes that are important in the pursuit of long-term goals.

We attend to those things in our surroundings and on our bodies that we deem important. The significant integrations that occur in the inferior parietal lobe suggest that all the information required to make such attentional decisions comes together here. Therefore, damage in this region can result in inattention also known as the neglect syndrome.

Damage to some portions of the frontal lobes can result in an opposite behavior. Patients may show increased attention to stimuli and can be impaired at disengaging from stimuli. If Hank had suffered from a right frontal lesion, he may have been aware of the chicken on the left side of the plate, but not the vegetables opposite the chicken on the right side of the plate—because he would have been unable to pull his attentional focus away, to disengage, from the chicken on left side of the plate.

Newberg and his coworkers at the University of Pennsylvania performed a functional imaging study on Tibetan Buddhists, who meditate by focusing on a mental image with clarity of thought and a loss of the awareness of space and time. We know that blood flow increases to the portions of the brain that are most active. The researchers found that during this focused meditation, blood flow to the frontal lobes increased. These results are very similar to those Newberg and his co-investigators (2003) reported in their study of Franciscan nuns who were performing meditative prayers.

Perhaps this frontal activation inhibits the sensory association areas and allows people who are meditating or praying to detach themselves from incoming environmental stimuli—and in keeping with some of our descriptions of spirituality, somehow to sense that they are part of something greater than themselves.

One way to have a spiritual experience (at least as we have talked about them) is to create a state of mind in which we withdraw attention from ourselves and our immediate surroundings and enlarge it into some more universal identity. Because the right parietal lobe is critical for focusing attention on both external stimuli and the self, developing the ability to have spiritual experiences might require reducing the activation of this area. The frontal lobes may enable this deactivation.

Studying patients with brain injury, Brick Johnstone at the Department of Health Psychology at the University of Missouri gave these patients a questionnaire that asked questions such as, "Have you ever had religious or spiritual experiences that changed your life?" He found that people with right parietal damage more often responded positively to these types of questions. Johnstone wrote, "This research also addresses questions regarding the impact of neurological versus cultural factors on spiritual experience. The ability to connect with things beyond the self, such as transcendent experiences, seems to occur for people who minimize right parietal functioning. This can be attained through cultural practices, such as intense meditation or prayer or because of a brain injury that impairs the functioning of the right parietal lobe."

## Doing Nothing: The Default Network

During functional imaging studies, participants may be asked simply to relax, rest, and do nothing; however, typically, they remain awake. The room is usually dark, with few or no sensory stimuli, and participants may be told to avoid focusing on or interpreting room sounds or any other sensory stimuli. The participants perform no actions and make no plans for actions. Raichle and his coinvestigators (2001) reviewed the brain images generated during this resting state and found that some areas in the brain still were active, including the middle (medial) structures of the cortex between the two hemispheres (Figure 9.3a) and the parietal lobes on both sides of the brain (Figure 9.3b). This medial cortex and parietal network is referred to as the default network.

We could not find reports of people having spiritual experiences while in a brain-imaging device. But in some respects, being in this kind of machine, without all the normal external stimuli of everyday life, is a bit like being in an isolation tank. Maybe this same default network is similarly active when people are in those isolation tanks and caves.

During many forms of prayer, contemplation, and meditation, we close our eyes. We are not conversing with anyone, nor are we planning any activities. In this state of mind, people will often spontaneously mull over past events and their interactions with others. Wendy Hasenkamp of the Emory University Department of Psychology along with her colleagues studied 14 breath-focused meditation practitioners. Even when attempting to focus attention on their breath, these meditators' minds wandered from their focus. To learn whether there was a change in activity in the default network during mind wandering, the researchers had the participants perform breath-focused meditation while in an fMRI scanner. If the subjects realized their minds were wandering, they were to press a button and resume focusing on breathing. Their brain imaging showed that during mind wandering, the default network was activated. It is likely that, when a person enters an isolation tank, or in more religious terms, enters the inner room and prays in secret, this same default network is activated.

The role of the default network in our prayers and during meditation, as well as its possible role in spiritual experiences, is not crystal clear, but studies of patients with brain injuries may provide us with some clues. Edward Valenstein, along with Ken and their colleagues at the University of Florida College of Medicine, published several papers about a patient with a cerebral hemorrhage in the back part of the default network known as the retrosplenial cortex. The cause of the hemorrhage was malformed blood vessels, which were surgically removed; unfortunately, though, the patient's retrosplenial cortex also was damaged. Examining the patient after surgery, Valenstein, Ken, and their coworkers discovered that his ability to recollect former memories and store

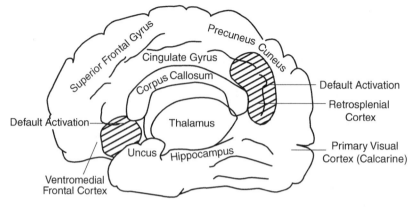

a.

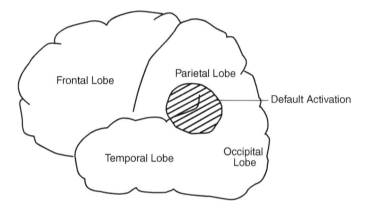

b.

*Figure 9.3* The default network: This network is active when a person lies in a machine
that is recording the alterations of blood flow in the brain, as in positron
emission tomography (PET) or functional magnetic resonance imaging
(fMRI). During this recording the person is resting and does not have to
attend to any stimulus or solve any problem. The default network includes
medial structures (Figure 9.3a) such as the ventromedial frontal lobe, the
posterior cingulate gyrus-retrosplenial area, the precuneus, and lateral structures such as the inferior parietal lobe (Figure 9.3b).

new ones was impaired. It turns out that this part of the default network is critical for memory recall. When someone is asked to rest and do nothing while in a
brain-imaging machine, this area involved with memory recall may be active. It
may also be active when a person is in a cave or a sensory isolation tank.

Several decades ago, Ken and his colleagues examined a woman who had
damage to both her left and right parietal lobes. As a part of her examination,

a picture of a Civil War scene was placed in front of her. When asked what she saw, the patient could only decipher parts of the image but not the whole thing. She was able to recognize individual objects, but could not assemble all these pieces into a meaningful, whole picture. Her parietal damage was in another portion of the default network. Marc Himmelbach, along with his coworkers from the Hertie Institute for Clinical Brain Research in Tübingen, Germany, published a paper describing a patient with a similar problem and whom they studied with functional imaging. They found that one of the areas critical to seeing the "whole picture" was in the medial parietal lobes (a region called the precuneus), which is also a part of the default network.

When an abnormal behavior appears after a part of the brain has been damaged, such as not being able to see the "big picture," we conclude that this same part of the brain, when healthy and undamaged, helps to normally mediate this behavior. We see that in the above examples: with lesions in the parietal lobes, the individuals could no longer see the big picture. With these observations, Ken proposed that during sensory isolation, a healthy default network, while still recalling memories, may also be aligning or organizing our many individual, unrelated memories into some more unified or meaningful picture.

If that seems a bit unclear, think about this example. We have talked before about the thread that unites as the basis for creativity, the finding of relationships among disparate things. Many great scientists, vexed by challenging problems, have been able to find unity in what appears to be diversity during those times when they were relaxing and alone, with minimal external interruption. What Ken was suggesting is that such scientists unknowingly may be tapping into their default network; then they see not unrelated elements, but more connected, meaningful information, which results in a novel solution to the problem at hand. It is conceivable that, in a similar way, activation of the same region may enable our attaining a greater, more unifying perspective on the minutiae of life, and the result may be a spiritual experience.

Our default network has another important structure we should discuss, the cingulate gyrus (Figure 9.3a). It appears to have a central role in integrating the areas in our brain that store knowledge and mediate our emotions. For example, it gets information from the amygdala when we are fearful or angry. It also has reciprocal connections with the frontal and parietal lobes, important to thinking and goal-oriented behaviors.

Robert Watson, Ken, and co-investigators from the University of Florida provided some interesting insight into one of the cingulate gyrus functions. We have seen that monkeys who were born in research laboratories, where no snakes are present, still have a fear of them. One such monkey, with the cingulate gyrus surgically removed from one half of the brain, was exposed to a toy snake in the visual field opposite the unoperated hemisphere. (Remember that, generally speaking, visual stimuli appearing on one side will be processed by the opposite side of the brain.) Seeing the snake, he showed the expected mix of fear and rage. But when the snake was shifted to the opposite side of his body so that the visual information projected to the hemisphere where the cingulate was removed, he showed no emotion.

We also have seen that the psychologist James Olds and Peter Milner (then a postdoctoral fellow) discovered a reward system (the ventral striatum including the nucleus accumbens) in the brains of laboratory rats that was so powerful that the rats would forgo food and water just to receive more of an electrical stimulus. The cingulate gyrus also has strong connections with this reward system, as do areas critical for memory. It is not surprising that addictive drugs also excite this system.

"The most beautiful and most profound emotion we can experience is the sensation of the mystical," said Einstein. Do prayer and meditation also activate this system and become addictive? Monks and others who are engaged in spiritual activities give up many earthly rewards and pleasures so that they can experience a continuing joy in spirituality.

## Seizures and Spirituality: Religious Experiences

Earlier we mentioned that functional imaging studies of the brain have revealed that when a person is having a visual hallucination, the portions of the brain normally important for actually perceiving such visual stimuli become active.

As we also discussed, nerve cells in a resting state are electrically charged; when stimulated by another neuron or by a sensory stimulus, such as a noise, the nerve cell discharges an electrical current travels down its branches, exciting neighboring neurons. Although this kind of discharge is integral to normal brain function, neurological disease and other factors can prompt uncontrolled firing, known as a seizure.

Seizures, like sensory deprivation and drugs, can cause hallucinations. The uncontrollable firing of neurons in the visual parts of the brain may give rise to visual hallucinations; should such misfiring occur in auditory portions of the brain, a person may hear sounds or voices that are not really there. When motor neurons similarly misfire, convulsions may result.

Evidence of trephination—the ancient therapy of drilling holes in the skull to treat epilepsy and other conditions—dates back some 10,000 years. Injury to the skull and brain can cause seizures, and removal of bone fragments and blood clots through these holes could have had therapeutic effect. Even frontier surgeons of the 1800s, such as Benjamin Winslow Dudley, used trephination to treat people with posttraumatic epilepsy. Indeed, Dudley reported that four out five of his patients who underwent this surgery recovered from the epilepsy.

The words *seizure* and *epilepsy* have similar meaning and the word epilepsy is derived from the Greek word *epilambánein*, which means "to get hold of, to attack." In the past, many people thought that convulsions were a sign that the person had been seized or taken hold of by the devil. Some historians have suggested that in earlier times, holes were drilled in the skull so that evil spirits could leave the person. Because this therapy actually worked in some cases, it seemed to confirm the idea that demonic spirits were being released. Hippocrates may have been among the earliest people to assert that epilepsy was not caused by possession. But even now, a curious relationship lingers between epilepsy and spirituality.

Over 150 years ago, two French doctors, Jean-Étienne Dominique Esquirol and later Bénédict Augustin Morel, were the first in the modern era to note a relationship among epilepsy, religiosity, and spirituality. Although this affiliation has been confirmed in more recent studies, the reason behind this relationship is not clear.

One of the more transparent explanations is that epilepsy is a disability that can work against having sustainable relationships. A person with epilepsy can find it harder to obtain and keep a job. There are many activities in which sufferers cannot participate, for if they have a seizure they might injure themselves and others. Epileptics often have a decreased sexual drive, which can make them less attractive to potential partners. And because a seizure can be a frightening event to witness, many of us might shy away from epileptics. People with epilepsy often are isolated; perhaps many epileptics turn to God out of loneliness. But this still would not explain why some individuals have sudden religious conversions after a seizure.

A famous story of a religious conversion is that of Saul, known to Christians as Saint Paul. Saul was from southeastern Asia Minor, in what is now Turkey. Born in the first decade of the common era (CE) to a Jewish family, he was educated in Jerusalem, where he became a Pharisee. The Pharisees were one of three major sects of Jews that arose several centuries before the birth of Christ, and they continued to be active several centuries after his birth. Priding themselves on their loyalty to God, they were extremely religious, meticulously followed all the Jewish laws, and despised anyone who deviated from them. Of all the opponents of Jesus and Christianity, the Pharisees were perhaps the most ferocious. As a Pharisee, Saul continuously and persistently persecuted members of the new Christian faith, which at the time almost completely consisted of former Jews. To rid the world of these wayward Jews who believed that Jesus was the Messiah, the high priest of the Temple in Jerusalem provided Saul with a military unit. Saul's plan was to travel to all the lands where Christians might be living, capture them, and bring them back to Jerusalem.

As illustrated on the cover of this book by Caravaggio's wonderful painting, Saul, traveling on the road to Damascus, suddenly fell to the ground, saw blinding lights, and heard a voice saying, "Saul, Saul why are you persecuting me?" Blind for three days afterwards, he recovered and traveled to Damascus, where he converted to Christianity, was baptized, and adopted the Greco-Roman name Paul. His lifelong goals changed, and he became a missionary, attempting to convert both Jews and gentiles to Christianity and preaching about Jesus, salvation, and resurrection.

This would not be the last of such episodes for Paul, nor was he alone among other religious leaders who apparently were also epileptic. The prophet Muhammad once said, "The revelation is always brought to me by an angel; sometimes it is delivered to me as the beating sound of the bell—and this is the hardest experience for me; but sometimes the angel appears to me in the shape of a human and speaks to me." Those close to the Prophet noted that during these states, he would remain motionless or move his lips. Sometimes he would have episodes of anxiety or fall to the ground with a shaking of his neck and shoulders.

The Prophet Muhammad, may have had a disorder called partial epilepsy with secondary generalization. Seizures that start in the amygdala (Figure 6.1), which is in the temporal lobe, often ignite a fearful state. Seizures that occur in the auditory or visual cortex may produce auditory or visual hallucinations, for example the "sound of the bell" or visions of angels. Lip movements and lip smacking are commonly observed in people with partial seizures.

Emanuel Swedenborg, born in 1688, was a brilliant scientist. Yet he is best known for his theology and his monumental, multivolume *Arcana Coelestia*, or in English, "Heavenly Secrets." As his religiosity blossomed, he abandoned his advanced but not well-recognized scientific activities. He wrote "I have been called to a holy office by the Lord himself, who most mercifully manifested himself in person to me his servant in the year 1743, when he opened my sight to the view of the spiritual world and granted me the privilege of conversing with spirits and angels, which I enjoy to this day. From that time I began to print and publish the various arcana that have been seen by me or revealed to me, concerning heaven and hell, the state of man after death, the true worship of God, the spiritual sense of the Word."

It appears that Swedenborg's "eyes were opened" during episodes that very well could have been partial seizures. Many of the things he described are typical of temporal lobe epilepsy, including seeing auras, falling, loss of consciousness, convulsions, visual and auditory hallucinations, trancelike states, and, afterward, mental confusion and memory loss.

The Hebrew prophet Ezekiel; Siddhartha Gautama, the Buddha; and the founders of the Society of Friends (Quakers), Shakers, and Mormonism, George Fox, Anne Lee, and Joseph Smith, respectively, all showed signs of epilepsy. But how common are these religious experiences in general? Orrin Devinsky and George Lai of the Department of Neurology at the NYU School of Medicine have estimated that 3 to 4 percent of people with partial epilepsy have religious experiences.

Postictal and interictal religious experiences occur most often in those people with temporal lobe epilepsy. These religious experiences occurred in 1.3 percent of all epilepsy patients and 2.2 percent of TLE patients. Many of the epilepsy-related religious conversion experiences occurred postictally. Often, before they lose awareness, patients with partial-seizure or temporal-lobe epilepsy have an aura. These occur because the cells in one of the areas in the temporal lobe are beginning to fire inappropriately. Depending on the side of the brain from which these seizures emanate, they often have different effects. For example, according to Devinsky and Lai (2008), seizure activity originating in the right hemisphere's temporal lobe more often gives rise to auras which can be visual or auditory hallucinations. According to Devinsky and Lai (2008), religious premonitory symptoms or auras were reported by about 4 percent of epilepsy patients, and patients with right temporal lobe epilepsy appear to be more likely to have these religious auras. In contrast, patients with left temporal lobe epilepsy are more likely to have increased religiosity and religious experiences between their seizures. Steve Waxman along with Norman Geschwind, who was the former Putnam Professor of Neurology at Harvard, along with coworkers noticed that patients with left-temporal-lobe seizures often wrote excessively, sought out the most profound meanings of life, and had an increase of religiosity.[1] D. Frank Benson, who was trained by and worked with Geschwind at the Boston Veterans Affairs Hospital, wrote a paper in which he called this group of behaviors the Geschwind Syndrome.

As mentioned earlier, the onset of the loss of consciousness or convulsions associated with a seizure a patient with epilepsy can have an aura, which while part of the seizure, this aura experience, may produce ecstatic experiences and feeling of being overcome by the divine. Reporting on the Russian novelist Fyodor Dostoyevsky's epilepsy, the French neurologist Théophile Alajouanine (1963) offered this quote by the great Russian author: "People can't imagine the happiness which we epileptics feel during the second before our attack. For all the joys that life may bring, I would not exchange for this one. . . . [S]uch instances were characterized by supreme exaltation." Dostoyevsky also wrote, "I have really touched God. He came into me myself: yes God exists, I cried." The full neurological basis of such experiences remain a mystery. However, it appears that the reward center, where sensations of euphoria are most pronounced, plays a role. Portions of the medial temporal lobe, such as the hippocampus and amygdala, have connections with the nucleus accumbens–ventral striatal reward center. Seizures that originate in these areas of the temporal lobe can activate this center. In his *Journal of Dreams*, Swedenborg wrote about an experience he had during Easter: "Had also in my mind and my body a kind of consciousness of an indescribable bliss, . . . that if it had been in a higher degree, the body would have been as it were dissolved in mere bliss" (15, §48).

Those with epilepsy, like unaffected people, can have feelings of déjà vu, the sense that they have experienced something before. Kovacs and co-investigators performed a functional imaging study while a patient was experiencing a déjà vu. This study revealed that the right medial temporal lobe, including those areas that are normally important in storing memories, was activated during this seizure. If we have experienced something before, such an event can bring a comfortable sense of familiarity. The role of the right temporal lobe during feelings of comfort and familiarity was further advanced by studies of patients with a disorder known as Capgras syndrome. Having suffered from injury to their right hemisphere, such individuals will appear to have a deficit in familiarity. For example, a man with this disorder might be visited in the hospital by his wife. He might recognize his wife's face, but later this patient would tell the doctor that although the person who visited him looked just like his wife, this woman was really not his spouse. Despite the physical similarity, he would say he had the feeling this person was really a stranger. Such patients may come to these conclusions because they do not have the feeling of familiarity, comfort, and even joy that can come with seeing a loved one. Seizures that involve these areas in the right temporal lobe, whereby sensations of familiarity occur together with feelings of ecstasy, could conceivably engender a religious or spiritual experience.

Judaism and Islam forbid the use of icons, religious images, and statuary. In contrast, Christianity embraces iconography in all its forms. It is plausible that Saul, exposed to icons of Jesus, had stored these facial memories. Memories of faces are stored in the fusiform gyrus, which is located in the ventral (lower) portions of the temporal and occipital lobes, primarily on the right side (Figure 4.3). Is it possible that this same part of the brain is where Saul's seizure originated, inducing the hallucinations of Jesus and St. Paul's conversion to Christianity.

In a 1970 study, the British research psychiatrist Kenneth Dewhurst at Littlemore Hospital and the physician A.W. Beard at Middlesex Hospital described six patients who had religious conversions, apparently induced by temporal-lobe seizures. Like St. Paul, individuals with epilepsy might see the face and hear the words of Jesus. Experiencing such hallucinations along with feelings of ecstasy and the warmth of familiarity could ignite powerful religious emotions, like those attributed to Paul.

As mentioned above, patients with left temporal lobe epilepsy may display highly religious behaviors, but often without ecstatic religious experiences. The reason that religiosity is associated with left-temporal-lobe epilepsy is not known. One theory, proposed by James Willmore and Ken, is that when a person develops this devastating and unpredictable disorder and cannot find a reason for it, they might attribute their seizures to a supernatural power. In addition, because patients with epilepsy do suffer the consequences of this disease, some epileptics may view their disorder as a form of punishment and search for forgiveness.

## Note

1. Although right-temporal-lobe epilepsy is related to immediate religious conversions, patients with left-temporal-lobe epilepsy display highly religious behavior, but often without ecstatic religious experiences (Waxman and Geschwind, 2005). This increased religiosity may occur even in the absence of ecstatic seizures or seeing and hearing God. Many patients with left-temporal-lobe epilepsy are also hypergraphic (Waxman and Geschwind, 1974, 1975). Many of the leading religious figures we discussed earlier certainly were prolific writers.

# 10　The Greatest Fear

*I do not mind dying. I just do not want to be there when it happens.*
—Woody Allen

*All creatures tremble with fear in the face of death.*
—Gautama Buddha

Nearly 35 years ago, the primate research psychologist David Premack came to lecture at the University of Florida. He talked about teaching apes to use visual symbols as a means of communicating. He also demonstrated that chimpanzees can infer causation, a pretty sophisticated capability.

At a reception after the lecture, Ken had a chance to talk with him about forms of knowledge that require communication. Ken mention that almost all mammals appear to demonstrate fear of injury and death, and when in danger will either fight or take flight. Although their behavior suggests that they know they can die, they probably do not know that eventually they will die. Knowing that all animals are mortal requires the sharing of information. Although animals do have the ability to communicate, for the most part their communication deals with drives, such as sex and hunger, and with emotions, such as anger, fear, and love. Communicating the concept that all animal are mortal requires what has been called proposition language, so called because the proposition, communicated by sentences, can be determined to be right (correct) or wrong (incorrect). Without speech, reading, and writing, animals cannot express or communicate the proposition that all animals are mortal.

Spoken and written words are symbols of ideas. Because the visual symbols that Premack used with his studies also represent concepts, it would be possible to communicate propositions to these apes by employing these symbols.

While speaking with Premack, Ken wondered out loud about the interesting possibility of informing these apes that all animals—including apes—are mortal.

Ken remembers Premack grinning and saying that even if he could teach the apes this concept, he was not sure that he would want to. When Ken asked why not, Premack told him that if these chimps learned that they were all mortal and would one day die, they might spend all their time building a great ape and then praying to it—and no longer would be willing to participate his studies. That comment was worth more than a good laugh—it merited some serious consideration.

As Premack's response implies, one life event is certain and, for most of us, more frightening than any other: death. It is the standard by which all other fears are measured. When death happens, everything goes away, forever. Even imagining our ending is difficult, if not impossible. Yet, on the other hand, the 87 percent of the world's people who believe in a supernatural deity also hope for eternal life, do they not? Could such a hope be the underlying source of humanity's peculiar behavior—our yearning for the divine?

The famous psychologist B. F. Skinner, who brought behaviorism to world-wide attention, was convinced that almost all behaviors could be produced or controlled by providing the proper stimuli and then rewarding the desired behavior and not rewarding unwanted behaviors. Taking this theory to its ulti-mate conclusion would meant that animals and people would have to perform an action and then get feedback about its consequences before they can learn whether or not it would be desirable to continue with it.

During a guest lecture at the University of Florida in 1981, Skinner talked about the inevitability of a nuclear holocaust. He said that without experienc-ing the devastating effects of such a horrific event we could not and would not modify our bellicose behavior. He concluded by telling the audience that people will not act to preserve the world until it is too late. He also expressed the feeling that he did not see any hope. Skinner was neither a neurologist nor a neuropsychologist and appeared to be unaware of the functions of the frontal lobes. The Russian neuropsychologist Alexander R. Luria, whom we cited in an earlier chapter, performed both clinical observations and studies of those suffering from frontal-lobe injury. Luria's work showed that the frontal lobes play an essential role in our capacity to predict the future on the basis of cur-rent and past events and behaviors. This ability can prompt us to modify our actions to help ensure better future outcomes. Remember that our farmer Lee knew that if he wanted to provide food for his family then he needed to plant during the spring and he would have to harvest his crops in the fall. Lee also was aware that not planting would have negative consequences. Contrary to Skinner's concerns (and although it sometimes seems not to be the case), we do not have to perform an act to understand the potential of its consequences.

What's more, we can talk and share ideas. The development of propositional language allowed us to communicate and learn about things beyond our personal experience. Certainly one of those things is that we are mortal. No matter what someone has done in life, and no matter how lofty or admirable, he or she will die. Even though activities such as exercise, eating properly, taking vitamins and antioxidants, seeing a doctor for regular check-ups, and taking prescribed medicines may prolong our lives, life will still end. Death remains inevitable.

The development of self-preservative behaviors is essential to the survival of each species. We know that certain portions of the limbic systems, such as the amygdala, are important for mediating the emotions of anger and fear and for producing fight-or-flight behaviors. But the brain networks that give rise to the fear of death and the seeming instinct for self-preservation are not as well understood. We are aware, however, that humans are well endowed with such a neural system and that for most of us, this fear of death provides a very strong internal motivating stimulus. Knowing that danger may lurk in the future, our minds steer us out of harm's way.

Awareness of mortality starts fairly early in life. Ken's older daughter, Nicole, was four years old, and his son David was six, when they lived in a house where the master bedroom was some distance from the children's rooms. In the event that the kids needed Mom and Dad or some emergency developed, the rooms had been connected via an intercom system so, under some circumstances, Ken and his wife, Patricia, could hear their children's conversations.

Ken can recall hearing Nicole ask David a rhetorical question: "Do you know that some day Mommy and Daddy will die and some day we will be dead?" David replied, "Yes. So what? You die and then you are born again and this happens over and over again."

Now, Patricia was raised as an American Baptist Christian, whereas Ken was brought up as a Reformed Jew. Because neither of these religions teach reincarnation, both were quite surprised by David's response. Patricia looked at Ken with a puzzled expression and asked, "Did you teach him that?"

"No," he said. "You studied Judaism and know that we don't teach reincarnation. What's more, I do not believe in it."

"Okay then, you better go to their rooms and straighten them out," she said, still mystified.

"If you know the truth, you straighten them out," he said. "I do not know the truth, but if this belief gives them comfort, why should I straighten them out, or even say anything?"

According to Jean Piaget, one of the world leading child-developmental psychologists, children around Nicole's age are gaining an understanding of themselves as autonomous beings and opening to a new world of possibilities. They learn they are independent of their parents and other family members as well as the rest of the universe. They discover that they are mortal and begin developing their spirituality, a belief in God, and concerns about an afterlife. Youngsters at this stage become aware of their vulnerability and discover that Mom and Dad are not all-powerful, so they look toward a loving and all-powerful protector-God.

Given our innate fear of death, perhaps Blaise Pascal's simplified logic is reason enough to maintain our belief in God. Pascal, the famous seventeenth-century French mathematician, physicist, and theologian who helped develop probability theory, put forth a statistical-probability argument for belief in God. We might call it the "everything to gain, nothing to lose proposition." He suggested that in regard to God's existence, there are two possibilities: either God exists or God does not exist. If he does exist, there would be a heaven, and believing would allow a person to be rewarded with eternal bliss. If God exists but we do not believe, then two outcomes are possible: we might still be able to enter heaven, but then again, we might not. If, however, there is no God, there would be no heaven. With these possibilities, a person increases his or her probability of going to heaven by having faith in God's existence. Of course, by this logic, why should anyone not believe?

In the end, the evidence is pretty clear. Like all members of the animal kingdom, we have evolved the capacity for self-preservation; however, unlike other members of the animal kingdom, we alone behave as if there is a supreme deity. Indeed, humans are a peculiar species. But what if, beyond mere self-preservation, we have also evolved our very sense for the divine—for God itself?

# References

Abramowitz, J. S., Deacon, B. J., Woods, C. M., and Tolin, D. F. Association between Protestant Religiosity and Obsessive-Compulsive Symptoms and Cognitions. *Depression and Anxiety* 20, no. 2 (2004): 70–76.

Ahs, F. A., Pissiota, A., Michelgård, O., Frans, T., Furmark, L., Appel, L., and Fredrikson, M. Disentangling the Web of Fear: Amygdala Reactivity and Functional Connectivity in Spider and Snake Phobia. *Psychiatry Research* 172, no. 2 (May 15, 2009): 103–8.

Alajouanine, T. Dostoiewski's Epilepsy. *Brain* 86, pt. 2 (June 1963): 210–18.

Alexander, G. E., DeLong, M. R., and Strick, P. L. Parallel Organization of Functionally Segregated Circuits Linking Basal Ganglia and Cortex. *Annual Review of Neuroscience* 9 (1986): 357–81.

Angeles, P. A. *Dictionary of Philosophy*. New York: Harper & Row, 1981.

Arita, H. Anterior Prefrontal Cortex and Serotonergic System Activation During Zen Meditation Practice Induces Negative Mood Improvement and Increased Alpha Band in EEG. *Rinsho Shinkeigaku* 52, no. 11 (2012): 1279–80.

Austin, J. H. *Zen and the Brain: Toward an Understanding of Meditation and Consciousness*. Cambridge MA, MIT Press, 1999.

Balbuena, L., Baetz, M., and Bowen, R. Religious Attendance, Spirituality, and Major Depression in Canada: A 14-Year Follow-up Study. *Canadian Journal of Psychiatry* 58, no. 4 (April 2013): 225–32.

Bannon, S., Gonsalvez, C. J., and Croft, R. J. Processing Impairments in OCD: It Is More than Inhibition! *Behaviour Research and Therapy* 46, no. 6 (June 2008): 689–700.

Barnett, L. *The Universe and Dr. Einstein*. Mineola, NY: Dover Publications, 2005.

Baron-Cohen, S., Leslie, A. M., and Frith, U. Does the Autistic Child Have a 'Theory of Mind'? *Cognition* 21, no. 1 (1985): 37–46.

Barrett, J. L., and Johnson, A. H. The Role of Control in Attributing Intentional Agency to Inanimate Objects. *Journal of Cognition and Culture* 3, no. 3 (2003): 208–17.

Baxter, L. R. Brain Imaging as a Tool in Establishing a Theory of Brain Pathology in Obsessive Compulsive Disorder. *Journal of Clinical Psychiatry* 51, no. 2 suppl. (February 1990): 22–25.

Beauregard, M., and Paquette, V. Neural Correlates of a Mystical Experience in Carmelite Nuns. *Neuroscience Letters* 405, no. 3 (September 25, 2006): 186–90.

Bechara, A., Tranel, D., Damasio, H., Damasio, A. R. Failure to Respond Automatically to Anticipated Future Outcomes Following Damage to Prefrontal Cortex. *Cerebral Cortex* 6, no. 2 (March–April 1996): 215–25.

Bench, D. J., Friston, K. J., Brown, R. G., Scott, L. C., Frackowiak, R. S., and Dolan, R. J. The Anatomy of Melancholia—Focal Abnormalities of Cerebral Blood Flow in Major Depression. *Psychological Medicine* 22, no. 3 (August 1992): 607–15.

Benson, D. F. The Geschwind Syndrome. *Advances in Neurology* 55 (1991): 411–21.

Benson, H., and Stark, M. *Timeless Healing: The Power and Biology of Belief.* New York: Scribner, 1996.

Berg, E. A. A Simple Objective Technique for Measuring Flexibility in Thinking. *Journal of General Psychology* 39 (1948): 15–22.

Berman, K. F., Ostrem, J. L., Randolph, C., Gold, J., Goldberg, T. E., Coppola, R., Carson, R. E., Herscovitch, P., and Weinberger, W. R. Physiological Activation of a Cortical Network during Performance of the Wisconsin Card Sorting Test: A Positron Emission Tomography Study. *Neuropsychologia* 33, no. 8 (August 1995): 1027–46.

Blumenthal, J. A. Depression and Coronary Heart Disease: Association and Implications for Treatment. *Cleveland Clinic Journal of Medicine* 75, no. 2 suppl. (March 2008): S48–53.

Boatman, D. J., Freeman, E., Vining, M., Pulsifer, D., Miglioretti, R., Minahan, B., Carson, B., Brandt, J., and McKhann, G. Language Recovery after Left Hemispherectomy in Children with Late-Onset Seizures. *Annals of Neurolology* 46, no. 4 (October 1999): 579–86.

Borg, J, Andrée, B. Soderstrom. H., and Farde, L. The Serotonin System and Spiritual Experiences. *American Journal of Psychiatry* 160, no. 11 (November 2003): 1965–69.

Broca, P. Remarques sur le siege de la faculte de la parole articulee, suives d'une observation d'aphemie (perte de parole). *Bulletin de la Societe d'Anatomie* 36 (1861): 330–357.

Bronowski, J. *Science and Human Values.* New York: Harper & Row, 1972.

Brownell, H., Griffin, R., Winner, E., Friedman, O., and Happe, F. Cerebral Lateralization and Theory of Mind. In S. Baron-Cohen, H. Tager-Flusberg & D. Cohen (Eds), *Understanding Other Minds: Perspectives from Developmental Cognitive Neuroscience,* 2nd edition (pp. 306–333). Oxford: Oxford University Press, 2000.

Bucky, P. A., and Weakland, A. G. *The Private Albert Einstein.* Riverside, NJ: Andrews McMeel, 1992.

Canessa, N., Gorini, R., Piattelli-Palmarini, M., Danna, M., Fazio, F., and Perani, D. The Effect of Social Content on Deductive Reasoning: An fMRI Study. *Human Brain Mapping* 26, no. 1 (2005): 30–43.

Carlsson, I., Wendt, P. E., and Risberg, J. On the Neurobiology of Creativity: Differences in Frontal Activity between High and Low Creative Subjects. *Neuropsychologia* 38, no. 6 (2000): 873–85.

Chamberlain, S. R., Blackwell, A. D., Fineberg, N. A., Robbins, T. W., and Sahakian, B. J. The Neuropsychology of Obsessive Compulsive Disorder: The Importance of Failures in Cognitive and Behavioural Inhibition as Candidate Endophenotypic Markers. *Neuroscience & Biobehavioral Reviews* 29, no. 3 (May 2005): 399–419.

Cohen, N. J., Eichenbaum, H., Deacedo, B. S., and Corkin, S. Different Memory Systems Underlying Acquisition of Procedural and Declarative Knowledge. *Annals of the New York Academy of Sciences* 444 (May 1985): 54–71.

Cook, N. D., and Hayashi, T. The Psychoacoustics of Harmony Perception. *American Scientist* (July–August 2008): 311.

Damasio, H. T., Grabowski, T., Frank, R., Galaburda, A. M., and Damasio, A. R. The Return of Phineas Gage: Clues about the Brain from the Skull of a Famous Patient. *Science* 264, no. 5162 (May 20, 1994): 1102–5.

Davidson, R. J. Anterior Cerebral Asymmetry and the Nature of Emotion. *Brain and Cognition* 20, no. 1 (September 1992): 125–51.

Dawkins, R. *The God Delusion*. London: Bantam Books, 2006.

DeLong, M. R., and Wichmann, T. Circuits and Circuit Disorders of the Basal Ganglia. *Archives of Neurology* 64, no. 1 (January 2007): 20–24.

Denny-Brown, D., and Chambers, R. A. The Parietal Lobe and Behavior. *Research Publications, Association for Research in Nervous and Mental Disease* 36 (1958): 35–117.

Dervic, K., Carballo, J. J., Baca-Garcia, E., Galfalvy, H. C., Mann, J. J., Brent, D. A., and Oquendo, M. A. Moral or Religious Objections to Suicide May Protect against Suicidal Behavior in Bipolar Disorder. *J Clin Psychiatry* (October 2011): 72(10): 1390–6.

Devinsky, O., and Lai, G. Spirituality and Religion in Epilepsy. *Epilepsy and Behavior* 12, no. 4 (May 2008): 636–43.

Dewhurst, K., and Beard, A. W. Sudden Religious Conversions in Temporal Lobe Epilepsy. *British Journal of Psychiatry* 117, no. 540 (November 1970): 497–507.

Divac, I., Rosvold, H. E., and Szwarcbart, M. K. Behavioral Effects of Selective Ablation of the Caudate Nucleus. *Journal of Comparative Physiology* 63, no. 2 (April 1967): 184–90.

Ekman, P., Wallace, V., and Friesen, W. V. Constants across Cultures in the Face and Emotion. *Journal of Personality and Social Psychology* 17, no. 2 (February 1971): 124–29.

———. The Repertoire of Nonverbal Behavior: Categories, Origins, Usage, and Coding. *Semiotica* 1 (1969): 49–98.

Epstein, J., Pan, H., Kocsis, J. H., Yang, Y., Butler, T., Chusid, J., Hochberg, H., Murrough, J., Strohmayer, E., Stern, E., and Silbersweig, D. A. Lack of Ventral Striatal Response to Positive Stimuli in Depressed versus Normal Subjects. *American Journal of Psychiatry* 163, no. 10 (October 2006): 1784–90.

Esquirol, J. E. D. *Maladies Mentales*. Paris: J.-A. Baillière, 1838.

Feinstein, J. S., Adolphs, R., Damasio, A., and Tranel, D. The Human Amygdala and the Induction and Experience of Fear. *Current Biology* 21, no. 1 (December 16, 2010): 34–38.

Fernander, A., Wilson, J. F., Staton, M., and Leukefeld, C. Exploring the Type-of-Crime Hypothesis, Religiosity, and Spirituality in an Adult Male Prison Population. *International Journal of Offender Therapy and Comparative Criminology* 49, no. 6 (December 2005): 682–95.

Feyman, R., Leighton, L., and Hutchings, E. *Surely You're Joking, Mr. Feynman!: Adventures of a Curious Character*. New York: W. W. Norton, 1997.

Foster, P. S., Valeria Drago, V., Webster, D. G., Harrison, D. W., and Heilman, K. M. Emotional Influences on Spatial Attention. *Neuropsychology* 22, no. 1 (January 2008): 127–35.

Gainotti, G. Emotional Behavior and Hemispheric Side of the Lesion. *Cortex* 8, no. 1 (March 1972): 41–55.

Gallagher, H. L., Happé, F., Brunswick, N., Fletcher, P. C., Frith, U., and Frith, C. D. Reading the Mind in Cartoons and Stories: An fMRI study of 'Theory of Mind' in Verbal and Nonverbal Tasks. *Neuropsychologia* 38, no. 1 (2000): 11–21.

Gardner, H. *Frames of Mind: The Theory of Multiple Intelligences*. New York: Basic Books, 1983.

Gazzaniga, M. S. Organization of the Human Brain. *Science* 245, no. 4921 (September 1989): 947–52.

Gazzaniga, M. S. The Split Brain Revisited, *Scientific American* (July 1998): 51–55.

Gervais W. M., and Norenzayan, A. Analytic Thinking Promotes Religious Disbelief. *Science* 27 no. 336 (April 2012): 493–6.

Ghacibeh, G. A., and Heilman, K. M. Progressive Affective Aprosodia and Prosoplegia. *Neurology* 60, no. 7 (April 2003): 1192–4.

Goldstein, K. *The Organism: A Holistic Approach to Biology.* New York: American Book Company, 1939; repr.: 1963.

Goleman, D. *Emotional Intelligence: Why It Can Matter More than IQ.* New York: Bantam Books, 1995.

Greenberg, B., and Shefler, S. Ultra-Orthodox Rabbinic Responses to Religious Obsessive-Compulsive Disorder. *Israel Journal of Psychiatry and Related Sciences* 45, no. 3 (February 2008): 183–92.

Griffin, R., Friedman, O., Ween, J., Winner, E., Happé, F., and Brownell, H. Theory of Mind and the Right Hemisphere: Refining the Scope of Impairment. *Laterality* 11, no. 3 (2006): 195–225.

Griffiths, R. R., Richards, W. A., McCann, U., and Jesse, R. Psilocybin Can Occasion Mystical-Type Experiences Having Substantial and Sustained Personal Meaning and Spiritual Significance. *Psychopharmacology* (Berl) 187, no. 3 (August 2006): 268–83.

Harlow, J. M. Recovery from the Passage of an Iron Bar through the Head. *Publ Massachusetts Med Soc.* 2 (1868): 327–347.

Happé, F., Brownell, H., and Winner, W. Acquired 'Theory of Mind' Impairments Following Stroke. *Cognition* 70 (1999): 211–40.

Harris, S., Kaplan, J. T., Curiel, A., Bookheimer, S. Y., Iacoboni, M., and Cohen, M. S. The Neural Correlates of Religious and Nonreligious Belief. *PLoS One* 4, no. 10 (October 1, 2009): e7272.

Hasenkamp, W., Wilson-Mendenhall, C. D., Duncan, E., and Barsalou, L. W. Mind Wandering and Attention during Focused Meditation: A Fine-Grained Temporal Analysis of Fluctuating Cognitive States. *NeuroImage* 59, no. 1 (January 2012): 750–60.

Hebb, D. O. The Effects of Early Experience on Problem Solving at Maturity. *American Psychologist* 2 (1947): 306–7.

Hebb, D. O. *The Organization of Behavior.* New York: Wiley, 1949.

Heilman, K. M. Intentional Neglect. *Front Biosci.* 9:(January 2004): 694–705.

Heilman, K. M. *Creativity and the Brain.* New York: Psychology Press, 2005.

Heilman, K. M., Bowers, D., Speedie, L., and Coslett, H. B. Comprehension of Affective and Nonaffective Prosody. *Neurology* 34, no. 7 (July 1984): 917–21.

Heilman, K. M., Bowers, D., Watson, R. T., Day, A., Valenstein, E., Hammond, E., and Duara, R. Frontal Hypermetabolism and Thalamic Hypometabolism in a Patient with Abnormal Orienting and Retrosplenial Amnesia. *Neuropsychologia* 28, no. 2 (1990): 161–69.

Heilman, K. M., and Valenstein, E. Frontal Lobe Neglect in Man. *Neurology* 22, no. 6 (June 1972): 660–64.

Heilman, K. M., Watson, R. T., and Valenstein, E. Neglect and Related Disorders. In K. M. Heilman and E. Valenstein (Eds), *Clinical Neuropsychology*, 5th ed., 296–348. New York: Oxford University Press, 2012.

Henig, R. M. "Darwin's God." *New York Times Magazine* (2007, March 4).

Himmelbach, M., Erb, M., Klockgether, T., Moskau, S., and Karnath, H. O. fMRI of Global Visual Perception in Simultanagnosia. *Neuropsychologia* 47, no. 4 (March 2009): 1173–77.

Idler, E. L., McLaughlin, J., and Kasl, S. Religion and the Quality of Life in the Last Year of Life. *Journals of Gerontology series B: Social Sciences* 64, no. 4 (June 2009): 528–37.

Iversen, S. D., and Mishkin, M. Perseverative Interference in Monkeys Following Selective Lesions of the Inferior Prefrontal Convexity. *Experimental Brain Research* 11, no. 4 (November 26, 1970): 376–86.

Izquierdo, A., Suda, R. K., and Murray, E. A. Comparison of the Effects of Bilateral Orbital Prefrontal Cortex Lesions and Amygdala Lesions on Emotional Responses in Rhesus Monkeys. *Journal of Neuroscience* 25, no. 37 (September 15, 2005): 8534–42.

James, W. *Varieties of Religious Experience.* Rockville, MD: ARC Manor, 2008.

Jeffries, K. J., Fritz, J. B., and Braun, A. R. Words in Melody: An H(2)15O PET Study of Brain Activation during Singing and Speaking. *Neuroreport* 14, no. 5 (April 15, 2003): 749–54.

Johnstone, B. Spirituality, Religion, and Health Outcomes Research: Findings from the Center on Religion and the Professions. *Missouri Medicine Quarterly* 106, no. 2 (March–April 2009): 63–66.

Kapogiannis, D., Barbey, A. K., Su, M., Krueger, F., and Grafman, J. Neuroanatomical Variability of Religiosity. *PLoS One* 4, no. 9 (September 2009): e7180.

Kaufman, Y., Anaki, D., Binns, M., and Freedman, M. Cognitive Decline in Alzheimer Disease: Impact of Spirituality, Religiosity, and QOL. *Neurology* 68, no. 18 (May 1, 2007):1509–14.

Kendler, K. S., Gardner, C. O., and Prescott, C. A. Religion, Psychopathology, and Substance Use and Abuse; A Multimeasure, Genetic-Epidemiologic Study. *American Journal of Psychiatry* 154, no. 3 (March 1997): 322–29.

Koenig, H. G. How Does Religious Faith Contribute to Recovery from Depression? *Harvard Mental Health Letter* 15, no. 8 (February 1999): 8.

Koenig, H. G., Hays, J. C., Larson, D. B., George, L. K., Cohen, H. J., McCullough, M. E., Meador, K. G., and Blazer, D. G. Does Religious Attendance Prolong Survival? A Six-Year Follow-up Study of 3,968 Older Adults. *Journals of Gerontology series A: Biological Sciences and Medical Sciences* 54, no. 7 (1999): M370–76.

Kovacs, N., Auer, T., Balas, I., Karadi, K., Zambo, K., Schwarcz, A., Klivenyi, P., Jokeit, H., Horvath, K., Nagy, F., and Janszky. J. Neuroimaging and Cognitive Changes during Déjà Vu. *Epilepsy & Behavior* 14, no. 1 (January 2009): 190–96.

Kret, M. E., Pichon, S., Grèzes, J., and de Gelder, B. Similarities and Differences in Perceiving Threat from Dynamic Faces and Bodies: An fMRI Study. *NeuroImage* 54, no. 2 (January 15, 2011): 1755–62.

Kuhn, T. S. *The Structure of Scientific Revolutions.* 3rd Ed. Chicago: University of Chicago Press, 1996.

Larson, E. J., and Witham, L. Leading Scientists Still Reject God. *Nature* 394, no. 6691 (July 23, 1998): 313.

Lee, G. P., Meador, K. J., Loring, D. W., Allison, J. D., Brown, W. S., Paul, L. K., Pillai, J. J., and Lavin, T. B. Neural Substrates of Emotion as Revealed by Functional Magnetic Resonance Imaging. *Cognitive and Behavioral Neurology* 17, no. 1 (March 2004): 9–17.

Lhermitte, F. Human Autonomy and the Frontal Lobes. Part II: Patient Behavior in Complex and Social Situations: The 'Environmental Dependency Syndrome.' *Annals of Neurolology* 19, no. 4 (April 1986): 335–43.

Lorenz, K. *Animal and Human Behavior*, Vols. 1 and 2. Translated by Robert Martin. Cambridge, MA Harvard. University Press, 1970, 1971.

Lunney, J. R., Lynn, J., Foley, D. J., Lipson, S., and Guralnik, J. M. Patterns of Functional Decline at the End of Life. *Journal of the American Medical Association* 289, no. 18 (May 14, 2003): 2387–92.

Lupien, S. J., Nair, N. P., Brière S., Maheu, F., Tu, M. T., Lemay, M., McEwen, B. S., and Meaney, M. J. Increased Cortisol Levels and Impaired Cognition in Human Aging: Implication for Depression and Dementia in Later Life. *Rev Neurosci.* 10, no. 2 (1999): 117–39.

Luria, A. R. Frontal Lobe Syndromes. In P. J. Vinken and G. W. Bruyn (Eds), *Handbook of Clinical Neurology II.* New York: Elsevier, 1969.

Mason, R. A., and Just, M. A. The Role of the Theory-of-Mind Cortical Network in the Comprehension of Narratives. *Language and Linguistics Compass* 3, no. 1 (January 1, 2009): 157–74.

Mayberg, H. S., Lozano, A. M., Voon, V., McNeely, H. E., Seminowicz, D., Hamani, C., Schwalb, J. M., and Kennedy, S. H. Deep Brain Stimulation for Treatment-Resistant Depression. *Neuron* 45, no. 5 (March 3, 2005): 651–60.

Mayberg, H. S., Robinson, S. G., Wong, D. F., Parikh, R., Bolduc, P., Starkstein, S. E., Price, T., Dannals, R. F., Links, J. M., and Wilson, A. A., et al. PET Imaging of Cortical S2 Serotonin Receptors after Stroke: Lateralized Changes and Relationship to Depression. *American Journal of Psychiatry* 145, no. 8 (August 1988): 937–43.

Mennemeier, M. S., Chatterjee, A., Watson, R. T., Wertman, E., Carter, L. P., and Heilman, K. M. Contributions of the Parietal and Frontal Lobes to Sustained Attention and Habituation. *Neuropsychologia* 32, no. 6 (June 1994): 703–16.

Menon, V., and Levitin, D. J. The Rewards of Music Listening: Response and Physiological Connectivity of the Mesolimbic System. *NeuroImage* 28, no. 1 (October 15, 2005): 175–84.

Milner, B. *Laterality Effects in Audition. In Interhemsipheric Effects and Cerebral Dominance.* Edited by V. Mountcastle. Baltimore: Johns Hopkins Press, 1962.

Milner, B. Effect of Different Brain Lesions on Card Sorting. *Archives of Neurology* 9 (1963): 90–100.

Morel, B. A. *Traité des Maladies Mentales.* Paris: Masson, 1860.

Mountcastle, V. B. The Columnar Organization of the Neocortex. *Brain* 120, pt. 4 (April 1997): 701–22.

Murray, C. Jewish Genius. *Commentary* (April 2007).

Newberg, A., Alavi, A., Baime, M., Pourdehnad, M., Santanna, J., and d'Aquili, E. The Measurement of Regional Cerebral Blood Flow during the Complex Cognitive Task of Meditation: A Preliminary SPECT Study. *Psychiatry Research* 106, no. 2 (April 10, 2001): 113–22.

Newberg, A., Pourdehnad, M., Alavi, A., d'Aquili, E. G., and Nottebohm, F. Cerebral Blood Flow during Meditative Prayer: Preliminary Findings and Methodological Issues. *Perceptual and Motor Skills* 97, no. 2 (October 2003): 625–30.

Nielsen, J. M. The Cortical Components of Akinetic Mutism. *Journal of Nervous and Mental Disease* 114, no. 5 (November 1951): 459–61.

Nottebohm, F. Ontogeny of Birdsong. *Science* 167 (February 13, 1970): 950–56.

Olds, J., and Milner, P. Positive Reinforcement Produced by Electrical Stimulation of Septal Area and Other Regions of Rat Brain. *Journal of Comparative and Physiological Psychology* 47, no. 6 (December 1954): 419–42.

Olds, M. E., and Olds, J. Effects of Lesions in Medial Forebrain Bundle on Self-Stimulation Behavior. *American Journal of Physiology* 217, no. 5 (November 1969): 1253–56.

Penadés, R., Catalán, R., Rubia, K., Andrés, S., Salamero, M., and Gastó, C. Impaired Response Inhibition in Obsessive Compulsive Disorder. *European Psychiatry* 22, no. 6 (September 2007): 404–10.

Peyron, C., O'Connor, K. J., Cunningham, W. A., Funayaja, E. S., Gatenby, J. C., and Gore, J. C., et al. Performance on Indirect Measures of Race Evaluation Predicts Amygdala Activation. *Journal of Cognitive Neuroscience* 12, no. 5 (2000): 729–38.

Peyron, C., Petit, J. M., Rampon, C., Jouvet, M., and Luppi, P. H. Neuroforebrain Afferents to the Rat Dorsal Raphe Nucleus Demonstrated by Retrograde and Anterograde Tracing Methods. *Neuroscience* 82, no. 2 (January 1998): 443–68.

Phillips, A. G., and Fibiger, H. C. The Role of Dopamine in Maintaining Intracranial Self-Stimulation in the Ventral Tegmentum, Nucleus Accumbens, and Medial Prefrontal Cortex. *Canadian Journal of Psychology* 32, no. 2 (June 1978): 58–66.

Premack, D., and Woodruff, G. Chimpanzee Problem-Solving: A Test for Comprehension. *Science* 202, no. 4367 (November 3, 1978): 532–35.

Previc, F. H. The Role of the Extrapersonal Brain Systems in Religious Activity. *Consciousness and Cognition* 15, no. 3 (2006): 500–39.

Pujol, J., Soriano-Ma, C., Alonso, P., Cardoner, N., Menchón, J. M., Deus, J., and Vallejo, J. Mapping Structural Brain Alterations in Obsessive-Compulsive Disorder. *Archives of General Psychiatry* 61, no. 2 (July 2004): 720–30.

Rachman, S., and de Silva, P. Abnormal and Normal Obsessions. *Behaviour Research and Therapy* 16, no. 4 (1978): 233–48.

Raichle, M. E., MacLeod, A. M., Snyder, A. Z., Powers, W. J., Gusnard, D. A., and Shulman, G. L. A Default Mode of Brain Function. *Proceedings of the National Academy of Sciences* 98, no, 2 (January 16, 2001): 676–82.

Rizzolatti, G., Fadiga, L., Gallese, V., and Fogassi, L. Premotor Cortex and the Recognition of Motor Actions. *Cognitive Brain Research* 3, no. 2 (March 1996): 131–41.

Robinson, R. G., and Benson, D. F. Depression in Aphasic Patients: Frequency, Severity, and Clinical-Pathological Correlations. *Brain and Language* 14, no. 2 (November 1981): 282–89.

Rosenzweig, M. R., Krech, D., Bennett, E. L., and Diamond, M. C. Effects of Environmental Complexity and Training on Brain Chemistry and Anatomy: A Replication and Extension. *Journal of Comparative Physiology and Psychology* 55, no. 4 (August 1962): 429–37.

Ross, E. D. Nonverbal Aspects of Language. *Neurologic Clinics* 11, no. 1 (February 1993): 9–23.

Routtenberg, A., and Lindy, J. Effects of the Availability of Rewarding Septal and Hypothalamic Stimulation on Bar Pressing for Food under Conditions of Deprivation. *Journal of Comparative Physiology and Psychology* 60, no. 2 (October 1965): 158–61.

Samson, D., Apperly, A., Chiavarino, C., and Humphreys, G. W. Left Temporoparietal Junction Is Necessary for Representing Someone Else's Belief. *Nature Neuroscience* 7, no. 5 (2004): 499–500.

Saxe, R., Xiao, D. K., Kovacs, G., Perrett, D. I., and Kanwisher, N. A Region of Right Posterior Superior Temporal Sulcus Responds to Observed Intentional Actions. *Neuropsychologia* 42 (2004): 1435–46.

Saxena, S., Brody, A. L., Schwartz, J. M., and Baxter, L. R. Neuroimaging and Frontal-Subcortical Circuitry in Obsessive-Compulsive Disorder. *British Journal of Psychiatry* suppl. 35 (1998): 26–37.

Schjødt, U., Stødkilde-Jørgensen, H., Geertz, A. W., and Roepstorff, A. Rewarding Prayers. *Neuroscience Letters* 443, no. (October 2008): 165–68.

Schreck, C. J., Burek, M. W., and Clark-Miller, J. "He Sends Rain upon the Wicked": A Panel Study of the Influence of Religiosity on Violent Victimization. *Journal of Interpersonal Violence* 22, no. 2 (July 2007): 872–93.

Schur, E. A., Noonan, C., Buchwald, D., Goldberg, J., and Afari, N. A Twin Study of Depression and Migraine: Evidence for a Shared Genetic Vulnerability. *Headache* 49, no. 10 (November–December 2009): 1493–1502.

Schwartz, C. E., Wright, C. I., Shin, L. M., Kagan, J., Whalen, P. J., McMullin, K. G., and Rauch, S. L. Differential Amygdalar Response to Novel versus Newly Familiar Neutral Faces: A Functional MRI Probe Developed for Studying Inhibited Temperament. *Biological Psychiatry* 53, no. 10 (May 2003): 854–62.

Scoville, W. B., and Milner, B. Loss of Recent Memory after Bilateral Hippocampal Lesions. *Journal of Neurology, Neurosurgery and Psychiatry* 20, no. 1 (February 1957): 11–21.

Segerstrom, S. C., and Miller, G. E. Stress and the Human Immune System: A Meta-Analytic Study of 30 Years of Inquiry. *Psychol Bull.* (July 2004 ): 130(4): 601–630.

Shelton, P. A., Bowers, D., and Heilman, K. M. Peripersonal and Vertical Neglect. *Brain* 113, Pt. 1 (February 1990): 191–205.

Short, B. E., Kose, S., Mu, Q., Borckardt, J., Newberg, A., Mark S., George, M. S., and Kozel, F. A. Regional Brain Activation during Meditation Shows Time and Practice Effects: An Exploratory FMRI Study. *Evidence-Based Complementary and Alternative Medicine* 7, no. 1 (March 2010): 121–27.

Sica, C., Novara, C., and Sanavio, E. Religiousness and Obsessive-Compulsive Cognitions and Symptoms in an Italian Population. *Behaviour Research and Therapy* 40, no. 7 (July 2002): 813–23.

Simonton, D. *Origins of Genius: Darwinian Perspectives on Creativity.* New York: Oxford University Press, 1999.

Socolar, R., Cabinum-Foeller, E., and Sinal, S. H. Is Religiosity Associated with Corporal Punishment or Child Abuse? *Southern Medical Journal* 101, no. 7 (July 2008): 707–10.

Squire, L. R., Ojemann, J. G., Miezin, F. M., Petersen, S. E., Videen, T. O., and Raichle, M. E. Activation of the Hippocampus in Normal Humans: A Functional Anatomical Study of Memory. *Proceedings of the National Academy of Sciences* 89, no. 5 (March 1992): 1837–41.

Starkstein, S. E., Robinson, R. G., and Price, T. R. Comparison of Cortical and Subcortical Lesions in the Production of Poststroke Mood Disorders. *Brain* 110, pt. 4 (August 1987): 1045–59.

Swedenborg, E. *Arcana Coelesti.* New York: Swedenborg Foundation, 1977.

Terry, R. D. My Own Experience in Early Research on Alzheimer Disease. *Journal of Alzheimer's Disease* 9, no. 3 suppl. (2006): 117–19.

Tiihonen, J., Rossi, R., Laakso, M. P., Hodgins, S., Testa, C., Perez, J., Repo-Tiihonen, E., Vaurio, O., Soininen, H., Aronen, H. J., Könönen, M., Thompson, P. M., and Frisoni, G. B. Brain Anatomy of Persistent Violent Offenders: More Rather than Less. *Psychiatry Research* 163, no. 3 (August 30, 2008): 201–12.

Tucker, D. M., and Williamson, P. A. Asymmetric Neural Control Systems in Human Self-Regulation. *Psychological Review* 91, no. 2 (April 1984): 185–215.

Ungerleider, L. G., and Mishkin, M. Two Cortical Visual Systems. In D. J. Ingle, M. A. Goodale, and R. J. W. Mansfield (Eds), *Analysis of Visual Behavior.* Cambridge, MA: MIT Press, 1982.

Vaillant, G., Templeton, J., Ardelt, M., and Meyer, S. E. The Natural History of Male Mental Health: Health and Religious Involvement. *Social Science and Medicine* 66, no. 2 (January 2008): 221–31.

Valenstein, E., Bowers, D., Verfaellie, M., Heilman, K. M., Day, A., and Watson, R. T. Retrosplenial Amnesia. *Brain* 110, pt. 6 (December 1987): 1631–46.

van den Heuvel, O. A., d. der Werf, Y., Verhoef, K. M., de Wit, S., Berendse, S., Ch. Wolters, E., Veltman, D. J., and Groenewegen, H. J. Frontal-Striatal Abnormalities Underlying Behaviours in the Compulsive-Impulsive Spectrum. *Journal of the Neurological Sciences* 289, no. 1–2 (February 15, 2010): 55–59.

van den Heuvel, O. A., Veltman, D. J., Groenewegen, H. J., Cath, D. C., van Balkom, A. J., van Hartskamp, J., Barkhof, F., and van Dyck, R. Frontal-Striatal Dysfunction during Planning in Obsessive-Compulsive Disorder. *Archives of General Psychiatry* 62, no. 3 (March 2005): 301–9.

van Grootheest, D. S., Cath, D. C., Beekman, A. T., and Boomsma, D. I. Twin Studies on Obsessive-Compulsive Disorder: A Review. *Twin Research and Human Genetics* 8, no. 5 (October 2005): 450–58.

van Ness, P. H., Kasl, S. V., and Jones, B. A. Religion, Race, and Breast Cancer Survival. *International Journal of Psychiatry in Medicine* 33 (2003): 357–75.

Watson, R. T., and Heilman, K. M. Callosal Apraxia. *Brain* 106, pt. 2 (June 1983): 391–403.

Watson, R. T., Heilman, K. M., Cauthen, J. C., and King, F. A. Neglect after Cingulectomy. *Neurology* 23, no. 9 (September 1973): 1003–7.

Waxman, S. G., and Geschwind, N. Hypergraphia in Temporal Lobe Epilepsy. *Neurology* 24, no. 7 (July 1974): 629–36; *Epilepsy & Behavior* 6, no. 2 (March 2005): 282–91.

———. The Interictal Behavior Syndrome of Temporal Lobe Epilepsy. *Archives of General Psychiatry* 32, no. 12 (December 1975): 1580–86.

Willis, T. *Anatomy of the Brain and Nerves.* London, 1681.

Willmore, L. J., Heilman, K. M., Fennell, E., and Pinnas, R. M. Effect of Chronic Seizures on Religiosity. *Transactions of the American Neurological Association* 105 (1980): 85–87.

Winter, T., Kaprio, J., Viken, R. J., Karvonen, S., and Rose, R. J. Individual Differences in Adolescent Religiosity in Finland: Familial Effects Are Modified by Sex and Region of Residence. *Twin Research* 2, no. 2 (June 1999): 108–14.

Wulsin, L. R., Vaillant, G., and Wells, V. E. A Systematic Review of the Mortality of Depression. *Psychosomatic Medicine* 61, no. 1 (January–February 1999): 6–17.

Yellott, J. L. Probability Learning with Noncontingent Success. *Journal of Mathematical Psychology* 6 (1969): 541–75.

Yorulmaz, O., Gençöz, T., and Woody, S. OCD Cognitions and Symptoms in Different Religious Contexts. *Journal of Anxiety Disorders* 23, no. 3 (April 2009): 401–6.

# Index

Goleman, Daniel 98
Golin, Rosalind 88
Gould, Stephen Jay xiii
grasp reflex 69, 94
Greenberg, Benjamin 62
grief 77
Griffin, Richard 47
Griffiths, Roland 106
Guilford, Joy Paul 91
Guilford Alternative Uses Test 91, 95
gypsies, persecution of 82
gyrus/gyri 22, 23

habits, and religious observance 40, 61, 72
habituation phenomenon 109
hallucinations 105–8, 116–17
Harlow, John Martyn 64
Harris, Sam xii, 58–9
Hartford Institute for Religious Research 61
Hayashi, Takefumi 50
heart failure, effect of religiosity/ spirituality on 81
heart rate 73
heaven/hell, spatial relationship 32, 34, 39
Hebb, Donald 21
Heilman, Ken xiii; brain damage assessment by 66, 109; on brain imaging 4–5; on communication 2–3, 122–3; on emotional experiences 32; and epilepsy evaluation 83–4; and language acquisition 24; stroke damage assessment by 35–6, 37–8, 48–9, 110–12
hemispheric disconnection syndrome 5
Henig, Robin Marantz xiii
heparin 92–3
Heschl's gyrus 52
Hinduism 1; and the location of God 40
hippocampus 8, 10–11, 17, 25, 53, 81, 120; removal of 16
Hippocrates 3
Holocaust 82
homosexuals, persecution of 82
hormone system 74
Howell, Henry 92
hymns, effect of 50, 52; *see also* music; singing
hyperreligiosity, and OCD 61–2
hypothalamus 74

imagery: religious 120; *see also* hallucinations
images, stored 106
imprinting 13–15, 83, 90
independence 103
inferior frontal lobe 30
inferior parietal lobe 23, 114
inhibitory effect 23–4
insula 73, 74
insular cortex 74
intelligence testing 97
intent, belief in 31
intentional mode 65, 67
intentions, of others 26–7
invention and innovation 88–9
Islam 1; association with OCD 62; genocide within 83; on heaven 39; and the location of God 39; and religious imagery 120; and violence 86; *see also* Muslims
Iversen, S. D. 76n2
Izquierdo, Alicia 87

Jackson, John Hughlings 49–50
Jacobs, W. W. 57
James, William xii, 91
Jeffries, Keith 49, 55
Jesuit Order 104
"Jewish Genius" (Murray) 96–8
Jews: culture of 85; intelligence in 96–100; persecution of 82, 86; secular 100; *see also* Judaism
John Paul II (pope) 89
Johnson, Amanda 31
*Journal of Dreams* (Swedenborg) 119
Judaism 1; association with OCD 6; on heaven 39; and the location of God 39; mourning in 39; Orthodox observance of 48, 62; and religious imagery 120; rituals and holidays 99; *see also* Jews

Kapogiannis, Dimitrios 30
Kaufman, Yakir 81
kinesthetic memory 28
Kissinger, Henry 15
Koenig, Harold G. 77, 80–81

Lai, George 119
language: acquisition of 23–4; and communication 2–3; use of metaphor in 32; structure of 30–31